HANNIBAL
MISSOURI

HANNIBAL
MISSOURI
A BRIEF HISTORY

KEN AND LISA MARKS

THE
History
PRESS

First published 2011

ISBN 978-1-5402-2102-5

Library of Congress Cataloging-in-Publication Data

Marks, Ken.
Hannibal, Missouri : a brief history / Ken and Lisa Marks.
p. cm.
Includes bibliographical references and index.
ISBN 978-1-5402-2102-5
1. Hannibal (Mo.)--History. 2. Hannibal (Mo.)--Biography. I. Marks, Lisa. II. Title.
F474.H24M27 2011
977.8'353--dc22
2011009967

CONTENTS

CONTENTS

PREFACE

In the mid-1970s, J. Hurley and Roberta Hagood, prompted by the Marion County Historical Society, decided to do some research on the history of Hannibal, Missouri. Both in their sixties, they had just retired and moved back to Hannibal. They had met and married while attending Hannibal-LaGrange College in 1928 and lived most of their adult lives in Southern California.

Hurley and Roberta were very thorough in their research. Roberta wrote out all the information she gathered by hand, using thousands of index cards and tablets of paper along the way. Hurley sometimes used a typewriter.

Their first book, *The Story of Hannibal*, was released for the American bicentennial celebration in 1976. Only fifteen hundred copies were printed.

In the next twenty-five years, the Hagoods would continue to research and write. Oral histories were recorded, too; they were able to capture firsthand accounts and personal recollections from Hannibalians born near the turn of the century. Eventually, the Hagoods would author and coauthor eighteen published books on Hannibal's history, innumerable self-published and mimeographed works and numerous articles for periodicals about Hannibal and neighboring towns. Two antique Hannibal history books would also be reprinted with assistance from the Hagoods: the eleven-hundred-page *History of Marion County*, first published in 1884, and *Mirror of Hannibal*, first published in 1905.

By the late 1990s, the Hagoods decided they needed to donate their research library and papers so that others would have access to the files. According to Roberta, it was difficult to find a place to store the information. Literally tens of thousands of pieces of paper had been accumulated over the years. The Hagoods assisted the Hannibal Free Public Library in opening the "Missouri Room," a dedicated space that holds the precious history of Hannibal. The Missouri Room is the repository of microfiche of Hannibal papers from as early as the mid-1850s, row after row of binders containing documents submitted to the National Register of Historic Places, old city directories, maps, thousands of pertinent books and periodicals and, of course, Roberta's index cards. Because of space limitations in the Missouri Room, the bulk of the Hagood collection made its way by truckload to the University of Missouri–Columbia campus, where it is now part of the Missouri Historical Society archives.

Sadly, Hurley passed away in 2002. Roberta celebrated her 100th birthday on December 7, 2010 ("a date that will live in infamy"). At the time of this writing, Roberta continues to gather newspaper clippings and other information for her historical scrapbooks and writes articles for local publications. We enjoy talking with Roberta; she's sharp and has an amazing memory. Anytime anyone in Hannibal has a question about history, he or she is told, "You need to talk to Roberta!"

One of the reasons we came to live in Hannibal was our fascination with the town's colorful history. By reading the voluminous writings by the Hagoods and spending countless hours in the Missouri Room of the Hannibal Library, we absorbed Hannibal's remarkable past. We began to share the history of Hannibal with guests on our guided historic and Haunted Hannibal tours, but invariably there would be even more questions: How did Hannibal get its name? Where did the wealth come from to build so many large homes and mansions? What is that Gothic-looking building on Broadway? What happened here during the Civil War? What do you do during floods? We soon began to add even more historical information on our tours, especially the Haunted Hannibal tours. But it wasn't just visitors to our town who asked the questions; Hannibalians who had lived here all their lives told us that during our tours we gave information about Hannibal's history they had never known.

We quickly realized that there was a need in Hannibal to communicate the history of the town in a succinct manner. Questions that guests have about Mark Twain's life and childhood are easily answered at the wonderful Mark Twain Boyhood Home and Museum Complex, but there is nowhere to learn about the town's history other than the Missouri Room in the basement of the Hannibal Free Public Library. Twain was only in Hannibal for fourteen years; Hannibal will celebrate its bicentennial in 2019. There's so much more history in Hannibal than just Mark Twain and no easy way to share it.

We began to envision a book that would give a concise account of Hannibal's history. We knew we didn't need to produce an exhaustive, micro-detailed version—that had already been done in 1884, 1905 and 1976. But previous volumes written about Hannibal were either out of print or cost prohibitive to most. We believed that a brief history of Hannibal might be helpful.

We didn't know what we were getting ourselves into with the writing of this book.

You see, there's just too much wonderful information about this old town. The stories are so rich that they are nearly unbelievable. The characters who have passed through Hannibal over the years are amazing and complex. We struggled when writing this book because we knew that space would be limited, and we would have to choose to leave some goodies out. There are too many newspaper articles, too many volumes of information, too many of Roberta's index cards to whittle down into one brief tome. Here's an example: our friend Steve Chou is a well-respected Hannibal historian with an amazing collection of Hannibal memorabilia. He has more than eleven thousand photographs and images that he is happy to share with anyone interested. As we sat with him and began to go through his collection, it was nearly impossible to choose only seventy images to publish in this book.

Some who read this account of Hannibal's history may be disappointed that we left out information they believe to be important. We hope our dear reader will understand that we had to make some tough choices on what information to include; we simply had to be brief. There are many people important to Hannibal's history, including current Hannibalians, who have contributed immeasurably to the preservation and advancement of the town, and we wish we could provide each and every one their proper place in Hannibal's history and credit for their achievements. We apologize in advance for any egregious omissions. (Now we know why the Hagoods had to write so many books!)

We hope this book will inspire you to dig deeper and learn more about Hannibal. You might, as have others before you, feel drawn to be a part of this historic community. There seems to be something magical about Hannibal, as if the town is frozen in time, as if you can look back over your shoulder and see Tom and Huck making their way down to Bear Creek, fishing poles in hand. But set aside Twain and Tom and Huck for a moment (if that's possible to do in Hannibal) and you'll see that there's much more to Hannibal's history. Imagine the pioneers who first settled between these bluffs, the riverboat calliopes singing their tunes as they pulled into port, the smell of fresh-cut lumber. Imagine the *clop-clop-clop* of the horse-drawn carriages parading fashionable ladies down Broadway during the Gilded Age or the illumination of hundreds of lights strung over Main Street during the 1898 Fall Festival. Imagine waving to FDR, Truman or Carter when they appeared in town. Imagine the spectacle of a cast of eleven hundred people appearing in a pageant to commemorate Twain's 100th birthday or the relief that was felt when the newly installed floodgates saved downtown Hannibal in the spring and summer of 1993.

There is so much rich history in Hannibal, both pre- and post-Twain. It is a magical place. We hope that you will spend time exploring it for yourself.

ACKNOWLEDGEMENTS

What is presented here would not have been possible without the foresight of many Hannibalians, who began, more than one hundred years ago, to painstakingly record the remarkable history of Hannibal, Missouri. We are humbled to now be a small part of that effort.

Special thanks to our parents, Terry and Alice Marks, and our beloved sons, Jordan Young and Shea Marks. Also, to Frank Elmore, who has always been more of a brother than an uncle, thank you for always being there, for serving as mentor, sounding board and the voice of reason. We love you all so much.

Thank you to Ben Gibson, Jaime Muehl, Magan Lyons and the staff of The History Press. We appreciate your assistance with this publication.

Groups like the Missouri Historical Society, the Marion County Historical Society and the Friends of Historic Hannibal keep history alive, and we are grateful for their support, encouragement and assistance.

Thank you to Michael Gaines of the Hannibal Arts Council for his generosity of time and materials. You are the standard to which we all strive.

Hallie Yundt-Silver and the entire staff of the Hannibal Free Public Library work tirelessly to provide a rich learning environment for young and old alike. Thank you for providing the chance to travel back in time for hours on end in the Missouri Room.

We wish to thank the folks at the Hannibal Convention and Visitors Bureau for their continued support. Your warm greetings and smiling faces help set the tone for our guests' visits to Hannibal and make life much easier for all of us in the tourism industry.

To the staff of the *Hannibal Courier-Post*, the *Quincy Herald-Whig* and KHQA in Quincy, thank you for helping us get the word out.

We appreciate the opportunity Rich Heiser has given us to share Hannibal's history in the pages of *Hannibal Magazine*. Thanks so much, Rich.

Jim and Sheryl Love, we could not continue to pursue our lofty ambitions in Hannibal without your kindness in all areas. We only hope to repay you in kind along the way.

We appreciate the efforts of the staff of the Mark Twain Boyhood Home and Museum and are especially grateful to Cindy Lovell for giving us the chance to bring the shoes back to Hannibal.

If a picture speaks a thousand words, then Steve Chou can tell the history of Hannibal better than anyone. This book would not have been possible without Steve's willingness to share not only his amazing collection of photographs but also his knowledge of all things Hannibal. Steve, thank you so much. Thank you to Linda Chou, as well, for opening your home to us time and again.

Finally, to J. Hurley and Roberta Hagood, thank you. You led the way, blazed the trail, provided the road map and made sense of it all. Your tireless devotion in recording Hannibal's history is without equal. The legacy of your life's work made this book possible.

THE FOUNDING OF HANNIBAL

On the banks of the swirling dark waters of the Mississippi River, nestled in a valley between twin limestone bluffs, they paused to marvel at the view. First, Native Americans; then the French; next the Spanish; and, soon thereafter, first- and second-generation Americans. Sitting alongside the shore, watching the majestic river roll by, looking first toward the hill to the north and then turning to examine the bluff with its natural rock cliff jutting out over the water to the south, these explorers paused, certainly acknowledging the beauty of the area. This small valley would one day become known as "America's Hometown," Mark Twain's boyhood home and the birthplace of Hollywood stars, an admiral and the "Unsinkable Molly Brown." For many generations of Hannibalians, it would simply be a place to call home.

For centuries, Native Americans freely roamed the area of what is now northeastern Missouri. They would winter in the region, tribes of Fox and Illinois and Sac (Sauk) Indians traveling downriver from their northern territories and camping along the banks of the great river. The tribes would hunt and fish, canoe around the islands between the shores of the Mississippi and perform sacred rituals on the unusual geological formation now called Lover's Leap. No single tribe claimed the area as its own, but many would travel through the area as part of their nomadic traditions. The river was called *misi-ziibi* ("great river") by the Ojibwe (or Chippewa) tribe.

EXPEDITIONS OF THE MISSISSIPPI VALLEY

In early June 1673, a small band of explorers made their way to the valley between the limestone bluffs on their southward journey down the Mississippi River. Their leader, Father Jacques Marquette, was a Jesuit priest from Laon, France. Seven years earlier, Marquette had been sent by the French government to Quebec as a missionary to the indigenous people of the Americas; while there, members of the Illinois tribe told him stories of a great river route to the south. He requested and was granted the opportunity to investigate the mighty river. Marquette was joined by Louis Joliet and five French-Indians, also known as the Métis. Marquette and his crew departed from St. Ignace on May 17, 1673, and went on to record the first known exploration of the Upper Mississippi Valley.

Louis Hennepin, a Catholic priest of the Franciscan Recollect order, was also sent by the French to Quebec, arriving in 1675 as a missionary working with the Iroquois Indians. He began explorations of the region with another French explorer, René-Robert Cavelier, Sieur de La Salle. Together, they searched the wilderness south and west of the Great Lakes in an effort to establish a series of trading posts.

Hennepin was instructed by La Salle to plan an expedition that would begin at the headwaters of the Mississippi, turn southward and then make stops along the way to survey the lands along the river. On February 29, 1680, Hennepin began his journey by canoe with two men and a small dog, traveling slowly south down the cold river. The party was delayed by dangerous ice on several occasions, and travel was slow. On March 30, they made their way to a small water inlet on the western shore of the Mississippi. Here they repaired their canoe, held Mass and named the area Bay de Charles. (This distinction may have been to honor Charles II of England.) Thus, while celebrating Mass along the inlet of Bay de Charles, Hennepin and his crew became the first Europeans to come ashore in the area that is now known as Hannibal.

La Salle would continue exploration and complete a study of the Mississippi region. On April 9, 1682, upon his arrival at the mouth of the great river where the waters flow into the Gulf of Mexico, La Salle claimed possession of the entire Mississippi Valley in the name of France's Louis XIV, calling the territory "Louisiana" in honor of His Majesty the King.

France would use the new Louisiana Territory as an area for colonization in the New World, sending the first brave settlers to the region in the late

Franciscan priest Louis Hennepin holding Mass along the shores of the Mississippi River (at Anthony Falls), circa 1673, depicted in a 1905 Douglas Volk painting. Hennepin was the first recorded white man to step ashore in the area that is now Bay de Charles. *Courtesy Library of Congress.*

1600s. By 1732, it was estimated that five thousand Europeans and two thousand enslaved Negroes populated the territory, where the colonists established plantations and cultivated indigo, tobacco and rice.

A secret treaty was signed by France in 1762 transferring the land west of the Mississippi in the Louisiana Territory to Spain. England would receive the land east of the Mississippi from the French a year later.

In 1800, the Spanish government commissioned Don Antonio Soulard, a Frenchman working as the surveyor general for Spain, to formally survey and map Spanish Louisiana. Soulard was well versed in the history of Ancient Rome, as maps produced by Soulard during this exploration bear the names he culled from popular military leaders from that era. On his published map, Soulard renamed Bay de Charles "Scipio" in honor of the Roman general who was victorious in the Second Punic War. A small river in the area was named "Fabius" for Fabius Maximus, the Roman general known for his skill in retreat. A short distance farther downstream, he came across another small tributary that wound its way throughout the valley between the twin bluffs, flowing west from the Mississippi, and recorded the name of the creek as "Hannibal." (Hannibal, although defeated by Scipio in the Second

Punic War, is still believed to be the greatest of all Carthaginian military commanders.) Thus, it was Soulard's map from 1800 that first bore the name Hannibal, marking the first recorded instance of the name's use in the area.

Early Hannibal Settlements

After defeating the British in the Revolutionary War, the newly formed United States government acquired all the land up to the eastern shore of the Mississippi River. In 1803, U.S. president Thomas Jefferson successfully negotiated the purchase of the remaining area of the Louisiana Territory from Napoleon's France for the total sum of $15 million. Jefferson's Louisiana Purchase included more than 828,000 square miles of land and virtually doubled the size of the United States of America.

Beginning as early as 1795, while the area was still in the hands of the Spanish, settlers began to dot the landscape in and around Hannibal. Mathurin Bouvet, a French colonist who had settled first in Ste. Genevieve (another river town south of St. Louis), obtained two land grants from the Spanish government, one near Bay de Charles and one in what is now Ralls County, Missouri. He brought kettles and equipment to boil the natural spring water in these areas for their salt content. The high salinity in the mineral water, when boiled down, produced sufficient quantities of salt to justify manufacturing and transporting the salt to St. Louis; 250 to 300 gallons of distilled brine water could yield a bushel of salt.

However, Native Americans in the area continually harassed Bouvet, looting and burning his settlement when he left to take salt south to St. Louis. According to U.S. Land Commission records, in the spring of 1800 (during the period when Soulard was surveying the area), Bouvet was killed by area natives, and his body was burned in his log cabin.

Bouvet's two Spanish land grants were sold at public auction to Charles Gratiot on November 30, 1800. Gratiot, a Swiss immigrant, had made his wealth during the American Revolution as a fur trader and merchant in St. Louis; after the war, he became a confidant of William Clark and Meriwether Lewis, assisting them as a translator to the Spanish governor of the territory. After securing the Bouvet land grants, Gratiot petitioned the Spanish governor in St. Louis and was granted additional land he claimed was necessary to ensure the success of the salt-manufacturing operation, as the additional acreage would provide more firewood to stoke the salt furnaces. He traveled northeast to the location of Bouvet's settlement with grants totaling more than nine thousand acres of land, built a cabin and set out to begin to harvest salt.

Soon after his arrival, however, Charles Gratiot was faced with the same troubles that Bouvet had encountered: confrontation and harassment by Native Americans. Gratiot was eventually driven from the area, abandoning his Spanish land grants, never to return. Soulard himself was sent by the Spanish governor to survey the area where the salt mining had been attempted, but he also faced threats from the same hostile natives and was unable to complete the survey.

Others tried to mine salt and settle the area of Hannibal in the first decade of the nineteenth century without much success. One notable exception was a fur trapper named Campbell (first name unknown), who had secured a contract through René Auguste Chouteau and formed a trading post on Bay de Charles as early as 1811. Chouteau, who was well connected with both French and Spanish royalty, had assisted Pierre Laclède in the founding of the trading post St. Louis in 1764 and granted Campbell the contract to establish his northern post. Campbell successfully navigated sensitive negotiations with the Native Americans and was able to eventually trade with them. Bringing goods one hundred miles upstream from St. Louis, Campbell would then trade with the Native Americans, supplying them with sundries for their furs and pelts, which he could then take back to St. Louis and resell for profit.

The New Madrid Earthquake

On December 16, 1811, at 2:15 a.m., a mighty earthquake shook the center of the United States. The quake measured 7.7 on the Richter scale, making it one of the most violent quakes ever to be recorded. The epicenter was found to be in the boot-heel area of southeastern Missouri, near a small town named New Madrid. Its strength caused the Mississippi River to change course, appearing to flow backward for a short time, and opened a fissure so large that the Reelfoot Lake in Tennessee was formed, filling with water from the river's altered path. Residents of cities as far away as Pittsburgh, Pennsylvania, and Norfolk, Virginia, were awakened by intense shaking; church bells were reported to ring in places as far away as Boston, Massachusetts; and sidewalks were reported to have been cracked and broken in Washington, D.C. Over the next two months, six other quakes would hit the region, each measuring no less than 6.0. More than eighteen hundred aftershocks measuring 3.0 or greater were also recorded between December 1811 and March 1812.

An eyewitness to the New Madrid Earthquakes, Eliza Bryan, recorded the following account on March 22, 1816:

> *A very awful noise resembling loud but distant thunder, but more hoarse and vibrating…was followed in a few minutes by the complete saturation of the atmosphere, with sulphurious* [sic] *vapor, causing total darkness. The screams of the affrighted inhabitants running to and fro, not knowing where to go, or what to do—the cries of the fowls and beasts of every species—the cracking of trees falling, and the roaring of the Mississippi—the current of which was retrograde for a few minutes, owing as is supposed, to an irruption in its bed—formed a scene truly horrible.*

The settlement of New Madrid was destroyed. Residents in the area, who suffered the terror of hundreds of strong aftershocks and whose land had been rendered useless by the quake, petitioned Congress for relief. Three years later, on February 17, 1815, the New Madrid Certificates were granted by Congress. These certificates entitled the devastated landowners up to 640 acres anywhere in Missouri that was still unclaimed and open in the public domain.

After Congress passed the New Madrid Certificate Act, the actual New Madrid sufferers were, in nearly every instance, defrauded. Before they were made aware of the available certificates, unscrupulous land speculators came to the New Madrid landowners and offered forty to sixty dollars for their claims; once purchased, the speculators would redeem the claim for the full 640 acres.

However, not all New Madrid settlers were victims. Some who were approached by dozens of eager speculators begging to buy claims took advantage of the opportunity for cash and were reported to have sold their claims many times over. This activity led to endless litigation over ownership and property rights of the New Madrid Certificate claims that would stretch over the next two decades.

MOSES BATES AND THE FOUNDING OF HANNIBAL

In 1816, a young man named Moses D. Bates arrived in St. Louis from Virginia to seek his fortune. Bates was ambitious and driven; upon his arrival in St. Louis, his first step was to establish one of the first lumberyards in the city. Next, Bates began learning carpentry skills. Soon, his business flourished when he began to offer his services as a contractor specializing in new construction. One of Bates's first contracts was to build a home for General William Clark, who, after returning from his famous expedition with Meriwether Lewis, had been appointed governor of the Missouri Territory by Thomas Jefferson. Clark chose St. Louis to establish his headquarters and chose Bates to build his new home.

During this time, Bates heard that William V. Rector, United States surveyor general, was planning to survey the northeast area of the Missouri Territory. He immediately secured an assignment to become part of the survey team as a chain carrier. The survey team commenced work in 1817 and continued into 1818. While working on the survey, Bates met the fur trader Campbell and learned of his success in negotiating with Native Americans. He saw the potential of the primitive trading posts in the land around Bay de Charles and began to envision a bright new future for the area.

After the survey was complete, Rector's team returned to St. Louis. Wasting no time, Bates immediately engaged Jonathan Fleming, a friend and fellow carpenter, to travel upstream by keelboat to begin construction on the new settlement he envisioned. Robert Masterson, John Bobb, Sam Thompson and a Frenchman known as "French Joe" were also enlisted and agreed to follow Bates and Fleming to the new settlement several weeks later.

Bates chose a small patch of ground near the banks of the Mississippi to make his camp. (This small plot later became the southeast corner of Main and Bird Streets.) He and Fleming began to clear the land, chopping down trees and using the rough-hewn logs to construct a one-story, "double log" house chinked with mud. This structure would serve to store equipment and provide shelter. After the others arrived, a second cabin was built; eventually, the bachelors Bates and Fleming would occupy half of the first cabin, sharing it with the storage of their equipment, and the families would take over the newly built second cabin.

Moses Bates continued to have business dealings in St. Louis and traveled up and down the Mississippi between the two settlements. It was during one of these business trips to St. Louis that Bates was introduced to Thompson Bird. Bird was the son of Abraham Bird, who happened to have been issued New Madrid Certificate #379 for the loss of his land during the earthquake. The savvy Bates was able to convince Bird to redeem the certificate and stake a claim in the northeast portion of the territory, which would, of course, include Bates's two-cabin settlement near the river.

Thompson Bird, having power of attorney and authority from his father, Abraham, redeemed the New Madrid certificate for 640 acres covering parts of Sections 21, 28 and 29 in Township 57, Range 4. Once the claim was secured, he conveyed one-eighth interest in the land tract to Moses D. Bates and sold one-half interest to Elias Rector of St. Louis for $960.

The layout of the property acquired by Bird had left a narrow strip of land in Section 29 unclaimed. Major Taylor Berry, a citizen of Howard County, had received the transfer of New Madrid Certificate #425, which had originally been issued to Jean Baptiste Grimard. Berry used part of the certificate to claim the remaining tract of land in Section 29 (the rest of the claim was applied toward land in the western part of the Missouri Territory). Because of its unusual shape—having one narrow strip of land connecting to a large lot to the north—Berry's land became known as the Broad Axe tract, covering a section of the area that today includes Riverview Park, Pleasant Street, Section Street and Gordon Street. Major Berry immediately began to advertise for carpenters to bid on construction of log cabins on the site. He had no interest in personally relocating to the region but saw potential profit in selling finished homesteads to incoming settlers.

Both of the claims made with New Madrid Certificates were quickly challenged. Shortly after redeeming his New Madrid Certificate, Major Berry was killed in a duel; the title to the Broad Axe tract could not be found, and litigation from many different claimants arose. Thompson Bird, having sold half interest to Elias Rector, who then went on to convey his interest in the property to several others, caused similar confusion, as the survey and town plat Bird claimed to have filed in Pike County was never recorded and could not be found. Litigation over ownership of land claimed by these two certificates would not be officially settled until as late as 1833.

Despite the legal wrangling, settlement of the small hamlet continued. In 1819, the new village was officially surveyed, and "Hannibal" was adopted as its name. By this time, the stream originally named Hannibal by Soulard had come to be known as Bear Creek by the region's settlers because of the black bears that were sometimes seen sleeping in the hollow logs of fallen sycamore trees along the creek's bank.

The original survey of the town called for thirty-three square blocks, each containing eight separate lots. As soon as the lots were made available for sale by the land office in St. Louis, Moses Bates and Sam Thompson purchased all of Block 33, riverfront property between what are now Rock and North Streets.

Jacob M. Lowe was a slave owned by Moses Bates. Lowe accompanied Bates to Hannibal when he was fourteen years old. Thomas H. Bacon interviewed Lowe in 1874 and reported the conversation in his book, *Mirror of Hannibal*:

> *Lowe said that soon after arriving in Hannibal, Bates began to clear land... The same year he built a warehouse near the place where the Planters Hotel was later built on Main Street near the corner of Hill. This was a storage building for the articles of trade which he expected to obtain from the Indians, trappers, traders, and early settlers—furs, hides, dressed deer skins, moccasins, leggings, hunting shirts, beeswax, honey, etc. He shipped them to St. Louis. Bates did a fairly good business.*

Bates enjoyed peaceful interaction with Native Americans in the area surrounding the fledgling settlement of Hannibal. In 1819, a temporary encampment of both Sac and Fox Indians was established in the area near Bay de Charles, the tribes having moved south to hunt and make their winter camp. While in the area, the Indians were recorded to have frequented the new trading post Bates had established on the site of what is now Hannibal High School, where he sold and traded goods brought up to Hannibal from St. Louis.

DISCOVERY OF THE CAVES

During the winter of 1819–20, Jack Sims was hunting along the snowy bluffs located just south of Bear Creek. Spying a panther roaming the hillside, Sims tracked the panther, following its prints through the snow and up the steep terrain. The tracks led Sims to a small, dark opening in the side of the cliff. Thinking that the panther must have chosen to make its den in a crevice that receded into the limestone, he blocked the den's entrance with stones and branches and planned to come back with his brothers. Sims then returned to his home in the settlement of Saverton, just a few miles south of Hannibal.

Sims returned to the hillside the next morning, accompanied by Roderick and William Sims, J.H. Buchanan and several of his dogs. As they cleared away the stones and other debris blocking the opening, they found that it was not a panther's den, as originally thought, but an opening to a large cave. With torches, they entered the cave and discovered an incredible labyrinth of limestone. For many years after its discovery, locals called the area "Sims' Cave."

SLOW GROWTH

Moses Bates continued to build his trading post and encourage others to settle in Hannibal during the winter of 1820–21. Later that year, on August 10, 1821, Missouri achieved statehood and became the twenty-fourth state admitted to the Union. During this time, land in the northeast Missouri territory could be purchased for $1.25 per acre. In an effort to encourage more settlers to populate the region now that Missouri was an official state, the price of land was substantially reduced by the land offices in St. Louis, sometimes reaching as low as $0.50 per acre.

Mr. and Mrs. John S. Miller had arrived in Hannibal in 1819 and built a log cabin near the area that is now the intersection of Center and Main Streets. Soon after, they welcomed a daughter, born in 1820, the first white child born in Hannibal. Miller later became the first blacksmith in Hannibal, expanding his cabin to house his new enterprise.

Abram Huntsberry, a hatter from Tennessee, also settled in Hannibal in 1819. Another early Hannibal settler was Amos Gridley, who operated a "dram shop" (tavern). The Gridleys celebrated the birth of the second child born in Hannibal, their daughter, Teresa Gridley, born in 1821.

However, the confusion that arose over property rights and lack of clear titles to lots being offered in Hannibal, coupled with the constant fear of attack from hostile natives in the area, kept most potential settlers at bay. The February 25, 1847 edition of the *Hannibal Gazette* explained the sentiment that prevailed in early 1820s Hannibal:

[The growth of the settlement] *appeared to come to a stand. All kinds of croakings* [sic] *were put into requisition to disparage its growth. It was called a frog pond, a grave yard, and denounced as having no good titles.*

By 1826, there were rarely more than four or five families living in Hannibal at any given time, and those who did come usually didn't stay very long. John Miller and his wife lost their daughter only a year after her birth; not only was she the first white child born in Hannibal, but she became the first white death reported as well. In 1823, the Miller family moved to Galena, Illinois, after hearing that lead mines had been discovered in the area. Abraham Huntsberry also left Hannibal, moving back south to Tennessee after a year of hardship in northern Missouri.

Even Moses Bates began to eye opportunities outside Hannibal. In 1821, after his marriage to Martha Gash (whose family were early settlers of the South River region below Hannibal), Bates began to construct keelboats. These were long, narrow, flat barges that could be used in shallow rivers and canals to transport livestock and cargo.

He began this new venture after learning from his friend, John Miller, of the need for such transportation in Galena, Illinois. The lead mines that had recently been discovered in northwestern Illinois had begun to attract new settlers to the area, and the village of Galena (named for the technical term for sulfide of lead) was growing rapidly.

Bates began to envision the development of a fleet of keelboats that could provide transportation from Galena to St. Louis. Galena was situated on the banks of the Fevre River (also known as the Fever River and later renamed the Galena River). Although called "river," it was actually a small, shallow tributary of the Mississippi where keelboats, which were easy to navigate in shallow waters, would be the most effective means of transport. Bates moved his trading post from Hannibal to Galena and, with the drive and determination he'd showed in both St. Louis and Hannibal, took the upstart settlement by storm. He eventually speculated in land, sold goods in his new general store, constructed buildings, assisted in the survey and plat of towns, mined lead and operated his fleet of keelboats from Galena. In 1826, the small Illinois village had organized itself into an official town, with Bates as one if its principal residents.

The Steamboat Era Begins

Steamboats had been on the Mississippi as early as 1811 with the launch of the *Orleans* out of Pittsburgh, Pennsylvania. During that decade, there were approximately twenty steamboats navigating the Mississippi; by 1830, more than twelve hundred were making the rounds between Minneapolis and New Orleans.

On May 2, 1823, the first steamer to ascend the Upper Mississippi left St. Louis. This was the *Virginia*, a side-wheeler 118 feet long by 22 feet across. The mission was headed by William Clark, who, after serving as governor of the Missouri Territory, had recently been named superintendent of Indian affairs by U.S. president James Monroe. Joining Clark on the maiden voyage were Lawrence Taliaferro, who served as the U.S. agent of Sioux affairs; Giacomo Constantine Betrami, an Italian explorer who kept a journal of the excursion; Great Eagle, a Sauk tribal chief of the region; and Moses D. Bates.

This expedition must have had a profound impact on Moses Bates. Soon, yet another business venture began to take shape in Bates's entrepreneurial mind, and by 1825, Bates had achieved sufficient financial success through his various business interests in Galena to launch his most ambitious enterprise to date: the establishment of a steamboat line between St. Louis and Galena.

While on a business trip to St. Louis in the summer of 1825, Bates purchased a small side-wheeler, the *General Putnam*. The crew carried axes and would make frequent stops along the river to chop the wood necessary to make the steam that powered the vessel. Immediately, Bates and the crew of *General Putnam* made regular trips between the lead mines of Galena and the ever-growing port of St. Louis; on each trip, whether heading north or south, Bates would require that the ship pause for a short stop along the shores of Hannibal.

As other steamboats began to appear on the river, new settlers traveling the Mississippi discovered Hannibal and slowly began to gather on its shore. The census of 1830 reported thirty residents of the village. Moses Bates continued to contribute to the village's development, establishing a horse mill for grinding flour and corn in 1827. Construction was still made with rough-hewn logs, but a cluster of new cabins appeared and began to branch farther west away from the river.

Steam-powered "packet boats" like the one above would bring trade cargo and settlers in the early years of Hannibal's growth. *Courtesy Hannibal Free Public Library.*

Central Park was founded in 1858 from land set aside by Stephen Glascock for a public square in the 1836 plotting of Hannibal. The park is still in use today. *Courtesy Hannibal Free Public Library.*

On August 12, 1831, Thompson Bird supplied a quitclaim deed to Stephen Glascock for the land Bird had acquired with his New Madrid Certificate. Glascock, a proven businessman and an official of the newly formed Ralls County, eagerly took charge of the land. The 1871 *Polk's City Directory of Hannibal*, in its "History of Hannibal" section, reported that in 1832 town lots on Main Street between Bird Street and Broadway were available for purchase at ten dollars each.

Glascock conducted an official survey of the area, so detailed that it included the course of Bear Creek, and filed new plat records in Marion County on April 17, 1836. Glascock would submit additional filings in December 1836 and again in 1839, which expanded the area of Hannibal in all directions from the original plat of thirty-three square blocks.

THE RISE AND FALL OF MARION CITY

In 1821, an enterprising twenty-four-year-old named William Muldrow made his way to Missouri. When Missouri was granted statehood in August of that year, the United States government set aside the saline lands in the northeastern region as property of the state, to be leased and used as a source of revenue for the government. The old Bouvet salt lick at Spalding was one of the sites selected to remain state's property. Muldrow was able to secure the lease of the old Bouvet lands, and moving to the area, he immediately drilled a new well and began to distill the mineral water to manufacture salt.

Muldrow achieved great success with his salt-making enterprise and became well respected in the tiny community. In 1831, when plans for a new Presbyterian college were developed by Reverend James Gallaher, Muldrow was named a trustee of the new college. Believing Muldrow to be a man with proven business savvy, Reverend Gallaher assigned to Muldrow the task of securing funds for the construction of the new institution. Muldrow's success at recruiting investors for the new college exceeded expectations.

Muldrow soon realized that a similar campaign to recruit investors could be applied to other business ventures. He and Reverend Gallaher began to envision a grand new settlement that they believed could become the largest metropolis west of the Mississippi. They named their new development Marion City. Muldrow chose land along the banks of the great river just twelve miles north of the village of Hannibal. First, he surveyed and laid out his new town; next, he was able to persuade a small group of residents in the region to provide the money for the purchase of the land, which they did with enthusiasm.

The plat Muldrow submitted designated lots for churches, a college, a female seminary, schools, businesses, warehouses and an opera house. He began to advertise the lots for sale in papers as far east as Philadelphia, Boston and New York. He traveled to the East Coast and met with potential investors personally, and his charm and enthusiasm were infectious. Muldrow succeeded in selling more than $185,000 worth of lots in Marion City, most to land speculators sight unseen.

With newfound confidence, Muldrow planned to convert an old slough that was part of Bay de Charles into a canal that would provide access for shipping vessels directly into the center of Marion City. Further, he planned the first railroad west of the Mississippi, calling for "steam cars" to be brought to the area. The rails themselves would be made of wood.

William Muldrow was eventually able to sell more than five hundred lots of Marion City land to speculators back East. While some investors paid cash, others purchased lots on the condition that improvements such as hotels, steam mills and stores must be completed before full payment was made. Muldrow began construction immediately. The weather during the summer and fall of 1835 was favorable, and great progress was made. Steamboats began arriving daily, bringing carpenters, masons, coopers, blacksmiths and plasterers, who in turn brought their families and needed supplies to the area. Some of the buildings planned were fabricated in other cities such as Cincinnati and St. Louis and sent in sections by steamboat to be reassembled in Marion City. Muldrow even went as far as to pay $11,000 toward his own steamboat, the *Caledonia*, to transport additional goods and labor to Marion City.

The excitement generated by Muldrow's bold new plan made its success seem certain. "The proprietors of Marion City and the projectors of the railroad began operations at once," reported R.I. Holcombe in his *History of Marion County*, published in 1884.

> *The timber was cleared for the track of the proposed railroad and the grading begun. Subscriptions to the stock of the new enterprise were solicited from the people, and poured in very rapidly and in considerable quantities. The surveyors determined that the site of the town was below high water*

mark and the levee was ordered thrown up along a portion to the bank of the river…In the summer and fall of 1835 it seemed as if a golden age had fairly arrived…prices of all kinds of property rapidly advanced, and a general stimulus pervaded the whole country. The heads of the entire community seemed to be turned, and nothing seemed worthy of consideration aside from the schemes of speculation and money-getting. It was raining a golden porridge, and the people made haste to hold up their platters.

On December 26, 1835, William Muldrow wrote a letter to Moses D. Bates. Muldrow had heard of Bates's planning abilities and the success Bates had achieved in both Hannibal and Galena, and he wrote in an effort to solicit Bates's assistance with Marion City. Bates, citing other interests that required his attention, politely declined.

In the spring of 1836, the eager settlers who had purchased lots sight unseen began to arrive by steamboat to Marion City. Construction had only been underway for a few months, and as the immigrants stepped onto the shore where they had envisioned a bright new future, instead they found an incomplete wetland of a village built on sand and mud, swarming with mosquitoes. The buildings promised were mostly incomplete, forcing some families to sleep in tents on their small plots of land.

Further, the previous winter had been harsh, producing heavy snows in Wisconsin and Iowa. The spring of 1836 was cold and wet, with temperatures remaining cool throughout May. As the weather suddenly turned warm, the snows from the north began to rapidly melt and surge downstream. The sudden massive influx of melted snow flowed into the Mississippi and began to mix with northeast Missouri's unusually heavy, late spring rains.

Soon, residents noticed that the Mississippi River was slowly creeping into Marion City. Day by day, the shore would encroach a little further. Eventually, the river overwhelmed the town; it was soon apparent to all that Marion City was situated in a flood plain.

By June 1836, during the height of the flooding, the entire town was submerged. Muddy river waters and debris flowed into the second story of some buildings. At the time, there was no way to forecast weather predictions or river flood stages, nor were there sufficient means of communication to warn those living along the banks of the Mississippi of the northern waters coming their way. The residents of Marion City, including William Muldrow, were taken completely by surprise.

Then, as the floodwaters receded over the long, hot summer of 1836, malaria set in. Mosquitoes, unsanitary conditions, contaminated drinking water and the deep mud left behind by the retreating river brought sickness and death to Marion City. Those who could soon fled the town.

In their book *Hannibal, Too*, J. Hurley and Roberta Hagood wrote that Charles Dickens, the most popular English novelist of the Victorian era, immortalized the tale of Marion City in his 1843 novel, *The Life and Adventures of Martin Chuzzlewit*:

> *Charles Dickens, the English novelist, visited the United States…He used Marion City, in the stage of its history just after the 1836 flood, as a subject for a narrative in his novel,* Martin Chuzzlewit. *He called Marion City by the name of "Eden." In his story Martin Chuzzlewit and Mark Tapley met a man known as General Scadder who convinced them to settle in Eden. Their journey to Eden by steamboat is described and their arrival is vividly portrayed. The flood waters had just receded and instead of the promised paradise, they found mud, slime, remains of buildings, a few cabins, and a people scourged by ague and other disease.*

Muldrow implored the residents of Marion City to stay, promising levees to protect the development. He insisted that the town could be saved, citing the facts that Chicago was built on a swamp and St. Petersburg on a marsh. Most did not heed Muldrow's pleas.

William Muldrow in no way tried to swindle his investors; he truly believed in his vision for Marion City. Muldrow's only crime had been in underestimating the power of the mighty Mississippi and the vulnerability of that particular area of land chosen for the grand metropolis he'd envisioned.

Marion City would never recover from the flood of 1836. Some residents stayed on and tried to rebuild, but the area continued to be inundated by flooding. For many years, attempts were made to save Marion City, but ultimately the settlement was never incorporated and was unable to grow into anything more than a struggling village.

In 1849, William Muldrow boarded his steamboat *Caledonia* and made his way toward the promise of gold in California. Eventually, the entire settlement was abandoned. Marion City had proven to be a complete and utter failure. Today, the only thing that remains of Marion City is a single monument, a large boulder commemorating the location that simply reads, "Site of Marion City, 1835."

Some who fled Marion City migrated twelve miles south to Hannibal. Hannibalians welcomed them, provided shelter and shared their food supplies. Soon, the refugees were incorporated into the small town as official citizens. The grateful families would write to loved ones, singing Hannibal's praises and encouraging them to visit. Hannibal saw its numbers swell from the thirty residents recorded in 1830 to nearly five hundred in 1837, in large part because of the failure of the community of Marion City. The carpenters, masons and plasterers who came to the area to build Marion City began to apply their skills toward the construction of Hannibal, and the riverside settlement began to grow.

A St. Louis newspaper, the *Daily Missouri Republican*, reported the plight of Marion City in "Removing a City," published on November 16, 1841:

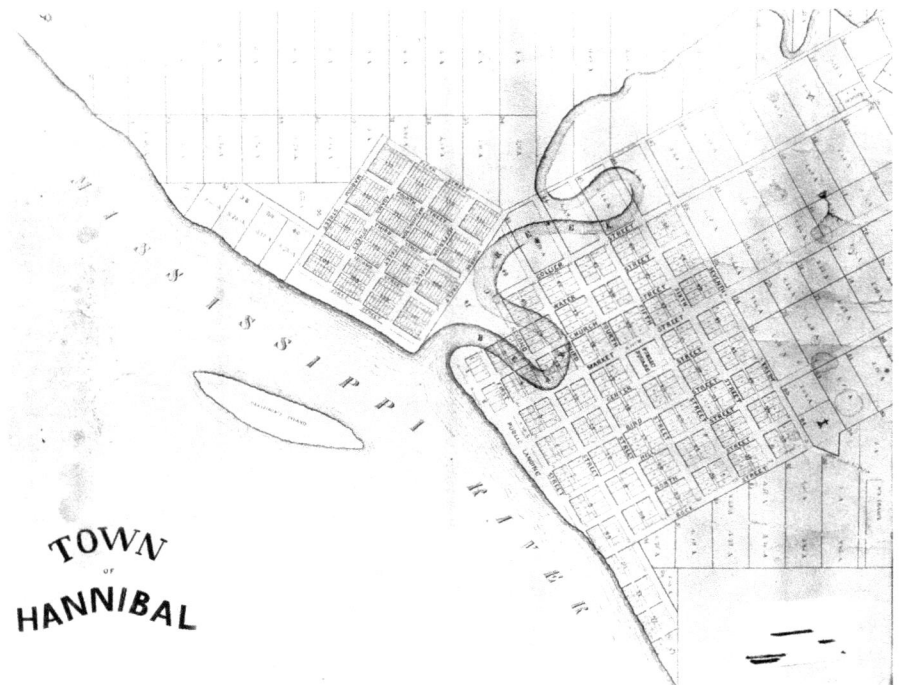

Hannibal in 1836. Bear Creek, as shown, was straightened years later to improve business on Main Street. *Courtesy Hannibal Free Public Library.*

The buildings of Marion City, on the Mississippi River, the same town in which so many eastern purchasers got their fingers burned a few years since, are being removed to Hannibal, a town some twelve miles below…When the buildings are removed to Hannibal they will be worth something, for there is no town on the Missouri side advancing more steadily and rapidly than this same place. Its business is already large in a commercial point of view, and within its limits is fast accumulating wealth, industry, population, and all the elements necessary to the creation of, in no distant day, a city.

New industries began to spring up in the village of Hannibal. Mr. Amelung of Cincinnati began operation of the first pork-packing plant in 1837, located at the river's edge on Market Street (now Broadway). A second pork-packing plant, operated by Shields and Williams, would also appear near the levee in 1838. Pork packing would prove to be one of the most important industries in Hannibal throughout the nineteenth century. As Bacon reported in *Mirror of Hannibal*:

The first marked prosperity arose with the pork and beef packing industry. As soon as the temperature sank enough, endless processions of hogs and cattle were headed for the tender mercies of the packing house. In those days the hogs ran free on the range and a hog had more rights than a man, since the porker could lawfully go wherever there was no lawful fence… On arriving in town a farmer's first question was comprised in a single word, "Wutsawgswuth."

During this time, the only reasonable method of transporting the hogs from farms to the packing plants was to drive them by foot. This meant that, on any given day, a large passel of hogs could be seen charging down Main Street toward the slaughterhouses situated near the levee. The squeals and bleating by themselves would produce quite a cacophony of sound; add to this the neigh of frightened horses, the bark of angry dogs, the pounding of hooves large and small on the packed dirt of Main Street and it is easy to imagine the chaos this parade of livestock could cause. On rainy days, the mud would be mixed with pig droppings and other eliminations, exacerbating the situation. Surely, the sidewalks and storefronts would clear quickly if one heard the ill-fated hogs coming his way.

Regardless of its shortcomings, the pork-packing industry generated growth throughout the village. Thousands of barrels were required to pack the meat for shipment by steamboats churning up and down the river, and cooper shops multiplied to build the needed wooden barrels. Salt production was increased, used to aid in the preservation of the meat. Labor was needed for these operations, and advertisements announced that jobs were available in Hannibal. With population growth came the need for new housing, larger general stores, blacksmiths and other necessary services. The increased revenue generated by these new industries spurred further growth. The promise of opportunity and prosperity encouraged many new families to move into the area and call themselves Hannibalians.

ANTEBELLUM HANNIBAL

1839: A WATERSHED YEAR

On March 1, 1839, after recording more than one thousand residents, Hannibal was officially incorporated into a town. A board of trustees was the form of government established, with Joseph Brasher named its first chairman of the board. One of the privileges granted to an incorporated town was the right to secure funds through taxation. Municipal services could then be established to improve the quality of life for Hannibal's residents.

In the ensuing spring and summer, Stephen Glascock began to make available to the public the lots he'd secured by quitclaim deed from Thompson Bird. They were sold in rapid succession. Hannibal became a frequent stop for steamboats churning up and down the river, and each year the boats arrived in greater numbers. Immigrants from all over the world arrived by steamboat to the shores of Hannibal. The growth of the new town was explosive.

In November 1839, a family of modest means that included five children and one slave moved from Florida, Missouri, into the Virginia House, a small hotel on Hill Street just east of Main. The new owner of the Virginia House, John Marshall Clemens, had purchased the entire block of Hill Street where the Virginia House stood for $7,000 from Hannibalian "Big" Ira Stout. Clemens was enthusiastic about relocating his family to Hannibal and optimistic about the opportunities for prosperity in the booming river town.

John Stobart's 1979 painting depicting Hannibal's Hill Street, circa 1841. *Courtesy Maritime Heritage Prints, John Stobart Galleries.*

The Clemens family included John Marshall; his wife, Jane; Orion, their eldest son, fourteen years old; their eldest daughter, Pamela, twelve; their son Benjamin, seven; their son Sammy, four; and Henry, the youngest son, just sixteen months old. Their teenage slave, Jennie, was the last of the slaves inherited by John Marshall Clemens from his Virginian parents, the other slaves having been sold previously to pay the family's considerable debts. Their arrival would forever change the course of Hannibal's history.

In the 1840 census, Hannibal recorded 1,034 citizens. This number would double by the end of the decade, making Hannibal the largest town in northern Missouri and third largest in the state. Two stagecoaches per day arrived in Hannibal, bringing news and visitors from Paris, Missouri, a small town forty-five miles to the west. The town also now had its first newspaper, the *Commercial Advertiser*, which was renamed the *Pacific Monitor* when J.S. Buchanan became the new publisher in May 1840.

New buildings began to spring up on the riverfront. The Pilaster House, a large, two-story frame building featuring large columnar "pilasters" on the front, was erected in 1840. Prefabricated in Cincinnati, Ohio, the Pilaster House was originally designed to be built in Marion City, where it arrived

Pilaster House (far right), constructed circa 1840. During Sam Clemens's childhood, Grant's Drugstore was located on the first floor. The Clemens family would live in the second-floor apartment for a time. Sam Smarr was murdered in front of the building in 1845, and John Marshall Clemens died here in 1847. Today, this building is part of the Mark Twain Boyhood Home and Museum Complex. *Courtesy Steve Chou.*

by steamboat in 1836. It was later moved to Hannibal and reconstructed at the southwest corner of Main and Hill streets by owner James Brady. Brick buildings also began populating Main Street—a drugstore, a general store, a tavern, a hotel. In October 1840, the First United Presbyterian Church began holding services in the first church building constructed in Hannibal on North Fourth Street between Bird and Hill Streets. Services at this church were attended by Jane Clemens and her young children, including ginger-haired Sammy.

Steamboats continued to arrive in Hannibal daily, always with great fanfare. As the ship would pull to shore, its magical calliope signing a tune, its whistle blowing, the town would become abuzz with excitement. Ron Powers, Pulitzer Prize–winning author who was born and raised in Hannibal, described the 1840s Mississippi River steamboat culture in his book, *Mark Twain: A Life*:

> *First, the deep coughing of the engines from perhaps a mile distant. Then a series of whistle blasts that echoed off the hillsides. Then the emergence from behind the bluff of the towering white emissary from Somewhere*

most unmistakably Else; first the prow of the three-tiered superstructure, the thirty-foot smokestacks pumping plumes of soot into the air; the high pilothouse and a figure at the knobbed wheel, staring ahead through the un-glassed window; and then the rest of the boat's curving three-hundred foot length, festooned with fluttering banners, pennants, the American flag; the boat's name written in bright decorative script across the paddle-wheel casing to break the whiteness.

If the steamboat docked at the levee, an expanse of inlaid stones, a land-locked local could glimpse a civilization unimaginable to one bred on the prairie at the nation's far rim: a civilization of chandeliers, brass fittings, draperied windows, and gold-framed mirrors; of red velvet carpets and gilded saloons and skylights of colored glass; a civilization of oil paintings and calliopes and great stacked bales of cotton to be exchanged somewhere for great stacks of money. A civilization inhabited by astounding diverse creatures. Strolling the decks or stepping onto the

The steamboat trade would continue in Hannibal even after the onset of the railroad system, especially with excursion boats such as the *St. Paul. Courtesy Hannibal Free Public Library.*

levee to stretch their legs were Southern planters in striped frock coats and wide-brimmed hats, their wives nearly invisible under deep bonnets, their floor-length silk dresses expanded by petticoat and restrained by corset; immigrants newly arrived from Europe at New Orleans; perfumed French merchants and high-hatted British speculators; expressionless gamblers in their ruffled blouses and jackets with velvet piping; mustachioed military men; assorted divines, actors, whores, circus troupes, politicians, trappers with their sidearms handy.

The steamboats brought with them to Hannibal news, entertainment and needed goods. They left with products produced in Hannibal, shipping the bounty to distant shores to be sold. The paddle-wheelers would then come about, turning to make the trip back to Hannibal from the other direction with loads of cash.

Hannibal was evolving from a muddy, homespun pioneer village to a civilized, modern, mid-nineteenth-century town. The steamboats, which provided a model of elegance and fine living, also brought with them news of the latest fashions and the goods to make one fashionable. Women adopted the use of hoop skirts; men sported fancy slouch hats, long dress coats and gold watch chains. Little girls were now seen wearing ruffled pantaloons and calico bonnets to shield their delicate skin from the glare of the noonday sun.

THE LEGEND OF LOVER'S LEAP

Lover's Leap is a 287-foot-high bluff of Burlington limestone that juts out over the Mississippi River to the south of Hannibal. The precipice was named long ago through the association of a famous urban legend perpetuated by Mark Twain's older brother, Orion Clemens.

In the early 1840s, while serving as a printer's apprentice, Clemens published the first mention of the tragic tale of Lover's Leap in Hannibal. As the story goes, two Indian lovers, a maiden from the Fox tribe and a young brave from the Illinois tribe, were prevented from marrying by their warring clans. The pair chose to jump to their deaths from the edge of the cliff and live together in eternity rather than be separated in life.

This legend was not necessarily invented by Orion Clemens. Winona, Minnesota was named after the legend of We-no-nah, an Indian maiden

Lover's Leap, as seen here circa 1880, offers a panoramic view of Hannibal. *Courtesy Steve Chou.*

who was believed to have plunged to her death after similar circumstances. Clemens may have heard the legend of We-no-nah from someone traveling from Minnesota on a steamboat down the river. Regardless of the legend's origin, once Clemens put the story into print, other Lover's Leaps suddenly sprang up across the country, with the story being told and retold with slight variations to fit the local terrain. As Mark Twain would say later in his book *Life on the Mississippi*, "There are fifty Lover's Leaps along the Mississippi from whose summit disappointed Indian girls have jumped."

SLAVERY IN LITTLE DIXIE

Despite the movement toward "civilization," it was not a happy-go-lucky existence for everyone in Hannibal. The Negro population of the town, whether slave or free, black or mulatto, was under constant watch, never allowed the opportunities of its white counterparts.

When Missouri was admitted to the Union as a state in 1821, slavery in the area expanded greatly. The Missouri Compromise of 1820 determined that Maine could join the Union as a "free state" (making the enslavement of Negroes illegal) and, in an effort to balance power in the Senate, allowed that Missouri be deemed a "slave state." Many slaveholders from Virginia and Kentucky moved into the region in search of new land specifically because they could maintain ownership of their slaves. A portion of northeastern Missouri became known as "Little Dixie" because of the volume of southerners who poured into the state after 1820.

When Hannibal was incorporated in 1839, one of the first acts of the new Hannibal Board of Trustees was "An Ordinance Respecting Slaves, Free Negroes, or Mulattoes," adopted just nineteen days after the board was first named. The ordinance prohibited certain activities by Negroes and outlined the punishment of both Negroes who broke the rules and whites who enabled them. There were eight sections adopted in the ordinance, covering everything from the wanton galloping of a horse through town by a Negro to the unlawful gathering of Negroes in groups greater than five.

Not everyone in Missouri was supportive of slavery, however. Abolitionists were present in the state and called for the slaveholding system to be abolished for the ultimate emancipation of every slave. Some hardcore abolitionists were inspired by religious fervor and were willing to break man-made laws they considered "immoral." They believed that, although slavery was legal in Missouri, helping slaves escape to freedom in the North was morally right, and thus they felt justified in ignoring slavery laws. Throughout Missouri, but especially in Little Dixie, abolitionists were feared and not welcome. As Bacon wrote in *Mirror of Hannibal*:

> *One fanatical, working "liberator" could set an entire county agog, and have whole neighborhoods up in arms; the greatest care and extreme vigilance were required and exercised to keep that one abolitionist out of the country, or to make his reception such that he would not care to return after being expelled.*

In July 1841, John Marshall Clemens was selected to sit on the jury of a very important slavery case, one that would send shock waves back East. The trial was held in Palmyra, the seat of Marion County. Three abolitionists—James Burr, George Thompson and Alanson Work—were being tried for aiding runaway slaves. The men were captured as they made their way back across the river to Missouri from Illinois, turned in to authorities by slaves who believed the white strangers were trying to get them in trouble.

In his book *Searching for Jim: Slavery in Sam Clemens's World*, Terrell Dempsey explains the drama surrounding the trial and the pressure on the jury to reach a favorable verdict:

> *Defendants Thompson, Work and Burr were charged with larceny—simple theft of property. The trial lasted for three days and drew the largest crowd ever to attend a trial in Marion County. Spectators filled the windows, hallway, and stairs leading to the courtroom and poured out onto the lawn. They were a boisterous group, and they made certain that everyone knew they were there for more than mere entertainment. If the result did not please them, they were prepared to take action.*
>
> *Respectable citizens said that if the court didn't punish the abolitionists, the mob would…The jury handed down a harsh sentence: twelve years for each man in the Missouri State Penitentiary.*

The verdict was criticized by pro-abolition publications across the country, such as the *Hartford* [Connecticut] *Observer*, which called Burr, Thompson and Work "Victims of Slavery." Defiant abolitionists immediately pronounced the three men martyrs and used the verdict as an example to recruit others to join the cause of emancipation. But the message being broadcast from the Marion County courthouse was clear: in Missouri, illegal activity by abolitionists would not be tolerated.

TIMES OF STRIFE AND MURDER

Living next to the great river was never an easy task. Each spring, the residents of Hannibal would keep an eye on the mighty Mississippi, as flooding was a constant concern. Some years, the river would rise to the point of overwhelming the levee and Main Street, causing temporary setbacks in the production and shipment of goods from Hannibal. Fortunately, Hannibal never suffered the devastation that Marion City had incurred due to flooding; the terrain of Hannibal was such that businesses and family homes just one block west of Main Street were on high enough elevations to prevent water from destroying the structures. Even during years of heavy flooding, the residents of Hannibal were able to overcome the damage left by retreating waters and resume their everyday lives.

Disease, however, was a serious issue, and illnesses such as cholera, measles and bilious fever sometimes threatened the entire town. Visitors arriving in Hannibal by steamboat sometimes carried with them viral infections, the high humidity and summer heat of the region made it a breeding ground for dangerous mosquitoes and the primitive forms of sanitation in use at the time also contributed to the spread of disease. Town streets were unpaved dirt (turning to mud during rains and flooding). Hogs, chickens, dogs and other animals were allowed to run free throughout the town, and horse droppings were everywhere. Physicians were ignorant to the spread of germs through contaminated utensils, and the medicines they distributed were mostly ineffective. Many Hannibalians lost their lives from disease throughout the nineteenth century. Even the Clemens family was not immune, losing nine-year-old Benjamin to a sudden illness in 1842.

In the fall of 1842, the voters elected John Marshall Clemens as Hannibal's justice of the peace. Proslavery Hannibal civic leaders had aided Clemens in his campaign, partially as compensation for his "favorable" service as a juror in the trial and conviction of the three abolitionists the previous year. The election to justice of the peace was gratefully accepted, as the Clemens family had fallen on hard times. During the abolitionists' trial, Clemens's dry goods store had failed, and he had lost all of his real estate holdings in Hannibal after creditors seized them for debt repayment. Even the Clemens's slave, Jennie, the last of the family's inherited slaves, had to be sold to pay the family's debts. Sadly, she was turned over to William B. Beebe, a businessman rumored to be a slave trader; Jennie was soon sent downriver into the Deep South.

After securing his new position, Judge John Marshall Clemens contacted his cousin, attorney James Clemens Jr. of St. Louis, and asked him for a loan of $330 to pay for the construction of a new home for the Clemens family. In the fall of 1843, Judge Clemens and his family moved into their newly completed home at 206 Hill Street. Today, the modest, two-story frame house still stands, famous throughout the world for being the boyhood home of Hannibal's most beloved son, Mark Twain.

On a warm September day in 1843, the first homicide occurred in Hannibal. Unfortunately for young Sam Clemens, it would be the first of many encounters with the dead during his childhood days in his beloved hometown.

That morning, Sammy had decided that it was too beautiful a day for any reasonable person to expect an eight-year-old boy to go to school. He stole away, truant. Sammy lollygagged the day away, fishing and creating his own adventures, and knowing he was going to be in trouble, he decided not to go home for dinner. After dark, Sammy was still nervous about going home, so he stayed out most of the evening. By midnight, he had made up his mind that he should accept his inevitable punishment by daylight and chose to sleep in his father's justice of the peace office and return home in time for breakfast.

Sammy climbed carefully in the window of the first floor of his father's office and crawled onto a "lounge" to go to sleep. Twain recalled many years later, in 1869's *The Innocents Abroad*:

> *As I lay on the lounge and my eyes grew accustomed to the darkness, I fancied I could see a long, dusky, shapeless thing stretched upon the floor…the pallid face of a man was there, with the corners of the mouth drawn down, and the eyes fixed and glassy in death!*

The victim was James McFarlane, a man who had been stabbed earlier in the day by the blade of an eight-inch knife. The accused was Vincent Hudson. The two Ralls County farmers had spent the day in Hannibal at a tavern, drinking. Later, while frequenting an implement store on Hill Street, they began to quarrel over the ownership of a plow. McFarlane lunged; Hudson pulled his knife.

The body had been taken to Judge Clemens's office, as he had planned to do his investigation and then to have McFarlane embalmed the next morning. Sammy had never made it home to hear that a murder had taken place in Hannibal that day, and he never dreamed he would curl up to go to sleep in his father's office lying next to a corpse!

Another murder, the first premeditated murder in Hannibal's history, occurred just over a year after the death of McFarlane. On January 22, 1845, a man by the name of Sam Smarr was casually walking down Main Street in front of Grant's Drugstore. His demeanor that day was misleading, however. Sam Smarr was known around town as a notoriously mean drunk. He had a propensity to talk trash when intoxicated, and sometimes in a particularly harsh way.

Justice John Marshall Clemens's law office, originally at 100 Bird Street. *Courtesy Hannibal Free Public Library*.

William P. Owsley owned a mercantile store directly across the street from Grant's Drugstore, just one block from the Clemens residence on the southeast corner of Hill and Main Streets. Sam Smarr had become obsessed with Owsley, making him a target of his drunken tirades on numerous occasions, saying that Owsley was a "damned son-of-a-bitch" (according to testimonies later taken by Judge John Marshall Clemens). Smarr accused

Owsley of swindling a considerable amount of money from the Thompson brothers in Palmyra, Missouri.

Owsley, who did not wish to dignify Smarr's accusations with a response, kept silent. Smarr continued to harass Owsley for several weeks. Apparently, on January 22, Owsley had had enough.

As Sam Smarr walked down the sidewalk in front of Grant's Drugstore, Owsley emerged from his mercantile. He crossed the street, called out, "You! Sam Smarr!" and drew a pistol from his pocket. Smarr turned; some people claimed to have heard him say, "Don't Fire!" Owsley ignored the plea, firing directly into Smarr's chest. He then paused to take aim again and fired a second shot.

Smarr fell but was not yet dead. Grant emerged from his store and, with the aid of several onlookers, carried Smarr into the drugstore and lifted him onto the counter. There, a crowd of curious townsfolk surrounded Sam Smarr and stood by and watched him die. Included in this gathering was nine-year-old Sammy Clemens.

Owsley was arrested for the murder, tried and acquitted; maybe the jury thought Smarr had it coming to him. However, after the acquittal, Twain wrote, "There was a cloud upon him—a social chill—and [Owsley] presently moved away."

During Samuel Clemens's boyhood throughout the 1840s and into the 1850s, Hannibal was very much the epitome of a Wild West frontier town. When Missouri achieved statehood in 1821, just fourteen years before Sammy's birth, it was considered the western edge of the nation. (Kansas would not become a state until 1861, and Oklahoma not until 1907.) The steamboats that populated the levee of the small river town brought to Hannibal's shores rough-languaged roustabouts, riverboat gamblers, land speculators, gold rush Forty-Niners and traveling minstrel show performers. (Thomas "Daddy" Rice himself appeared in blackface during a show in Hannibal in 1845, with ten-year-old Sam Clemens in the audience.) These colorful characters streaming to and from the steamboats on Hannibal's levee, some of whom would make their new homes in the small river town, would form a rowdy, and sometimes violent, sideshow of humanity.

From a Town to a City

On February 24, 1845, Hannibal was incorporated as a city, having been granted a charter by the State of Missouri after reaching a population of more than fifteen hundred souls. The government was turned over from the board of trustees to the city's first mayor, James Brady (who had constructed the Pilaster House at the corner of Hill and Main Streets in 1840). Hannibal now also had a recorder, an assessor and a city council.

Civic leadership in Hannibal began to have a major impact on the new city's future. In 1846, a public meeting was held in the office of Judge John Marshall Clemens. About a dozen people attended the meeting to discuss a new plan for Hannibal: the establishment of the Hannibal & St. Joseph Railroad. The group adopted the plan and asked Robert F. Lakenan, secretary of the committee, to prepare the charter immediately for presentation to the Missouri state legislature.

Although the small group had no experience and little knowledge of what was involved in building a railroad, it did have the foresight to know the impact the railway would have on the future of Hannibal. A rail line that cut directly across the state to the western city of St. Joseph would provide a route to ship Hannibal goods to markets in the developing West, possibly equaling the volume of goods currently being sent south by steamboat. It would take more than twelve years before the line was completed, but the small group of men from Hannibal, including the town's justice of the peace, was instrumental in securing a major transportation pipeline that would have an impact on Hannibal for more than a century.

By 1847, the booming river city was welcoming more than one thousand steamboats annually to its levee. Flour production had become big business in the area, with more than 110,000 bushels of wheat brought to Hannibal for milling and export that year. Other industries were thriving as well. Two hundred tons of hemp were used annually in Hannibal's ropewalks, with rope being a prime product manufactured in town. John Garth, who moved to Hannibal with his family in 1844, began a tobacco business and produced cigars and plug and chewing tobacco, exporting more than 400,000 pounds of products per year from his new facility. According to the February 25, 1847 edition of the *Hannibal Gazette*, a total of more than $1.2 million of goods had been produced in Hannibal the previous year.

Flour mills were some of the earliest businesses to take root in Hannibal, and the RoBards Mill, shown above, showcased its product at the 1853 World's Fair in New York. *Courtesy Hannibal Arts Council.*

The city was now home to twenty carpenters, fifteen physicians, fourteen wholesale and retail general stores, twelve attorneys, eight tailors, six brickyards, six blacksmiths, five cabinetmakers and undertakers, three hotels, three sawmills (one of them powered by steam), three saddle shops, two druggists, two watchmakers, two livery stables, a tanyard and a steam distillery. Amos and Brison Stillwell, who came to Hannibal in 1845, engaged in a new milling business at the mouth of Bear Creek. The Stillwells would also be involved with pork packing. Three hundred men were employed in the various pork-packing facilities along the levee, where, during a six-month period in 1847, thirteen thousand hogs and forty-five hundred cattle were slaughtered.

Although most Hannibalians were enjoying prosperity during this time, the Clemens family would experience a tragic turn of events in 1847. In early March, John Marshall Clemens traveled by horseback to Palmyra on

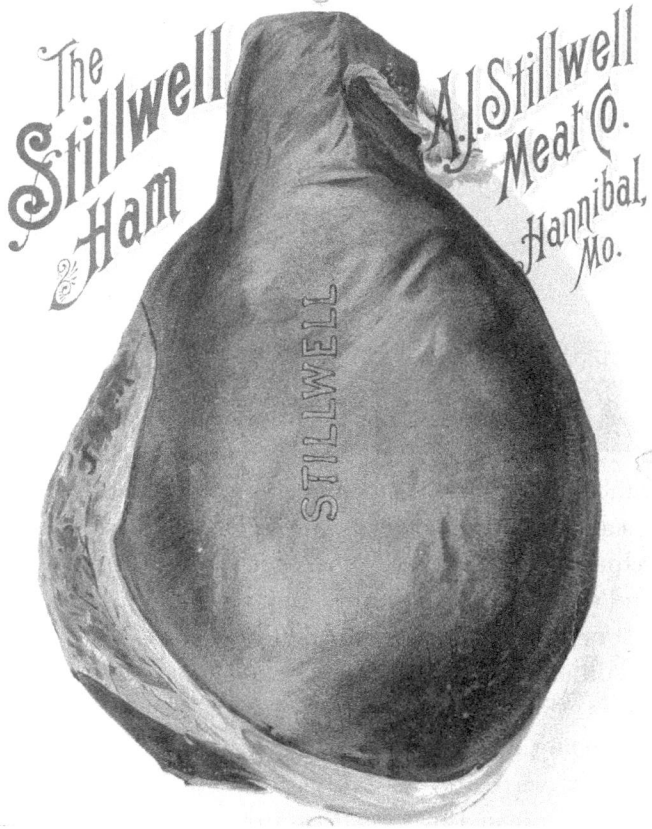

In addition to investing in the lumber industry, A.J. Stillwell owned a nationally prominent pork-processing plant. *Courtesy Steve Chou.*

court business at the Marion County courthouse. On his return, he rode the entire thirteen-mile trip in freezing rain. By the time he made it to Hannibal, he was feverish; eventually, the illness progressed to pneumonia. He was taken to a small apartment on the second floor of the Pilaster House above Grant's Drugstore, where he lay in delirium for nearly two weeks. On March 24, 1847, with his family around his bedside, John Marshall Clemens died.

His father's death thrust the eleven-year-old Sam Clemens into adulthood. He was obligated to begin earning an income, trying his hand first as a clerk in a general store, next as an assistant to a bookseller and then making deliveries for an apothecary shop. He tried to deliver papers for the *Hannibal Gazette*. He worked for a blacksmith. Finally, Sam's mother, Jane, spoke to Joseph P. Ament, publisher of the *Missouri Courier*, who agreed to take on young Clemens as an apprentice. Sam began by sweeping floors, fetching water and keeping the fireplace stoked in the winter. Eventually, Ament allowed Sam to learn to set type. The experience of preparing the type for printing by stringing together individual letters into words, and the words into sentences, would completely change Samuel Clemens's life.

THE ISSUE OF SLAVERY

In contrast to the advancement of Hannibal's white citizens, Negroes, both slave and free, continued to be oppressed. In Marion County, whose largest town was Hannibal, more than twenty-three hundred slaves were kept. In addition, forty-two "free" blacks were in residence, former slaves who were either able to purchase their freedom or were declared free in the last will and testaments of their now-deceased owners. These so-called "free" blacks were required to post bond and register with the city or county where they lived and were banned from most jobs, relegating them to work as sharecroppers or domestics right alongside non-free slaves.

Although Hannibal was not a major slave-trading center, there were slaves bought and sold throughout northeast Missouri. Advertisements frequently appeared in Hannibal newspapers offering slaves for sale or lease. Some advertisements were slave traders looking to buy slaves. Slaves were bought and sold by John Armstrong, who had an office and storeroom at the northeast corner of Center and Third Streets in the Melpontian Hall building. Orion Clemens (Sam's older brother), who then owned the *Journal and Western Union* newspaper in Hannibal, ran an advertisement by Francis Davis on August 14, 1851, advertising that Davis had "Cash for Negroes" and would pay the highest prices.

Another dichotomy of black and white culture in Hannibal could be seen in education. White children were being taught in both public and private schools in Hannibal, including the Hannibal Academy and Mary Newcomb's school in the basement of the Presbyterian church, where Sammy Clemens was sometimes a student. However, in 1847, the Missouri state legislature passed a law forbidding the teaching of Negroes or mulattoes, with the penalty of a $500 fine or six months' imprisonment. The fear was that, if taught to read and write, Negroes might be influenced by abolition literature smuggled into the community and would encourage one another to rise up in rebellion.

Two African American children photographed in J.R. Shockley's studio on Main Street during the Civil War. Hannibal, like much of Missouri, had diverging opinions on slavery by the onset of the Civil War. *Courtesy Library of Congress.*

While many in Hannibal supported this view, the city continued to have its fair share of abolitionists as well. As the question of slavery became more intense across the nation, tensions in town would also rise between the two factions. Quincy, Illinois, just across the river from Hannibal, was a destination for many runaway slaves moving north on the Underground Railroad; certainly, some runaways traveled through Hannibal in an attempt to reach Quincy. But as Sam Clemens would witness personally, not every runaway slave would make it to the promise of freedom across the river in Illinois.

On a hot August day in 1847, Sammy Clemens and his gang, which included John Briggs and Will Bowen, had made their way halfway across the Mississippi to fish and swim on Sny Island, a small patch of land and trees in the middle of the river.

Just a few weeks earlier, a young slave from the farm of Neriam Todd in Monroe County had run away and made it over to Sny Island on his way across the river to Illinois. He was discovered by Bence (also called Ben) Blankenship, the older brother of Tom Blankenship (Tom was Twain's inspiration for the character of Huckleberry Finn). At this time, anyone finding a runaway slave was considered heroic if he returned the slave to his/her owner; as a matter of fact, it was a crime not to. In addition, the Blankenship family was one of the poorest in the community, and along with the accolades Bence might receive, returning the slave would also fetch Bence a hefty reward.

Twain would recall Bence Blankenship's moral dilemma decades later as he began to work on *Adventures of Huckleberry Finn*. Just like the fictional character of Huck, Bence Blankenship chose to help the runaway slave rather than to selfishly turn him in for the reward. Bence began to make the dangerous journey across the river to Sny Island daily on his raft to bring food and supplies to the young Negro and would continue to do so for several weeks.

Eventually, however, word circulated that the runaway slave might be hiding on the island. A group of woodchoppers went across the river and over to Sny Island with the intent to capture the fugitive and return him for the reward. The group soon discovered the runaway, and while he was being chased toward an area of the island called Bird Slough, the young slave drowned.

Sammy and his friends had no thoughts of the slave on the hot day in August as they splashed and played at the water's edge on Sny Island. Soon, however, the boys' fun turned to sheer horror when, slowly rising from underneath the surface of the murky brown water, a face appeared. The runaway's mutilated body had been trapped by mud and debris in the river, and the boys' swimming had dislodged the corpse.

During the first week of September 1849, the first telegraph service was installed in Hannibal. Before, news had traveled slowly to Hannibal by way of steamboat, stagecoach or visitors on horseback and was therefore limited in scope. The telegraph brought news from all over the world to the shores of Hannibal, and one of the main topics coming over the wire was the issue of slavery. The debate had begun to rage across the nation, and it seemed every publication in the country chose a side, doing their best to influence their readership.

The tenor of everyday life in Hannibal began to change. More and more discussions turned toward the topic of slavery. Abolitionists, emboldened by the wave of antislavery sentiment emanating over the telegraph lines from the northeastern part of the United States, began to make themselves known, and clear lines began to be drawn between anti- and proslavery factions in Hannibal.

However, terrible tragedies would soon send Hannibal's abolitionists back "underground" and further strain tensions between the races in northeastern Missouri. The proslavery majority would use these tragedies to solidify its position in the community and force slaveholders to tighten their grip more fiercely in the years leading up to the Civil War.

In the fall of 1849, Thomas Glascock, a Marion County farmer, was working on a large building project and needed stone from a nearby quarry. He had hired another local farmer, William Callaghan, and Callaghan's slave, Isaac, to help with the excavation. Glascock's own slave, Ben, was responsible for driving the wagon back and forth between the quarry and the construction site.

On October 30, as Ben made his way through the woods, he noticed two white children playing and gathering nuts under a grove of large walnut trees. In a moment of absolute rage, and completely unprovoked, Ben jumped from his wagon. Reaching the small ten-year-old boy first, he grabbed a short, thick tree branch and struck the boy, probably killing him with the first blow. The boy's sister, a young girl of only twelve, was raped. After pulling his work knife from his pocket, Ben slashed the girl's throat and, not content to simply kill the girl, went on to mutilate the body.

Ben climbed back into the wagon and made his way to the quarry to retrieve the next load of stone. When he returned, Glascock sensed that something was amiss and, seeing blood on the slave's clothing, asked Ben why the return trip had taken so long. Ben, visibly shaken, claimed to be ill and suffering from a severe nosebleed. Glascock sent him home, believing the story because of Ben's disturbing demeanor.

The next morning, a farmer named Michael Bright reported his children missing. A search party began to comb the countryside. Later that day, the bodies were discovered, as was the knife used in the attack. It was quickly determined that Glascock's slave, who had been seen earlier with an identical knife, was the attacker. Ben was immediately apprehended for the crimes, and although he denied involvement and claimed he had lost his knife several days before the murders, he was arrested. Ben went peaceably, and the arrest was made without incident.

An unrelated but equally shocking event occurred just one week later. A group of slaves in Lewis County, the next county to the north of Marion County, planned an elaborate scheme to escape to the free soil of Iowa. Twenty-seven men, women and children belonging to four different white families banded together, stole wagons and weapons and prepared to make a mad dash to the Iowa border just thirty miles to the north.

On the morning of the escape, two of the white families began to suspect that something in their slave community was awry. After overhearing a conversation between slaves about the plan, one of the slave owners called for a posse to be raised, and some thirty armed white men gathered together. The posse soon learned that the slaves had congregated on the McCutchen Farm in Lewis County and set out to foil their escape.

The posse surrounded the slaves' hiding place and ordered them to lay down their weapons and surrender. They refused. Their plan was to escape, not fight, but they refused to yield. The slaves overturned their wagon as a shield and huddled behind it, clutching crude weapons such as pitchforks and wooden staffs. They did not understand that they were not only outnumbered by the posse but also out-gunned.

One of the older slaves, a man known only as John, broke the stalemate. He sprang from behind the wagon and charged toward the posse. Facing rifles with only a hay knife, John was immediately gunned down. The slaves heard the barrage of gunfire and realized the size of the group they faced. Knowing that the situation was hopeless and that their dreams of freedom were dashed, they reluctantly gave in to the posse and were returned to slavery.

The horrific murders of the Bright children, coupled with the Lewis County uprising, sent shock waves through the Hannibal community and set off a panic. Suddenly, whites who had owned slaves all their lives were terrified of them. The slaveholders feared that just beneath the surface, their slaves, slaves who helped raise their children, who tended their gardens and prepared their meals, might carry inside them the same murderous rage that Ben had demonstrated. The slaveholders had never before considered that their own slaves might harbor resentment that could grow into such vicious hostility; now they began to fear for their lives, worrying that domestic slaves might poison their food. Others were suspicious that field slaves, or slaves working with tools in pork-packing plants or blacksmith shops, might arm themselves and rise up in mutiny.

Glascock's slave, Ben, who showed no emotion or remorse throughout his incarceration and trial, was convicted of the heinous murders of the Bright children on December 4, 1849. He was put to death by hanging from hastily constructed gallows just north of Palmyra, near Joseph Sallee's mill, on January 11, 1850. It was the first legal execution in Marion County. The event was attended by residents of several Missouri counties.

The *Missouri Courier* (then the employer of fourteen-year-old apprentice Sam Clemens) reported on the execution. In its January 17, 1850 edition, the *Courier* estimated that the crowd included as many as ten thousand onlookers. "There was a deep feeling of resentment throughout our whole country, against the perpetrator of so horrid, merciless and unprovoked a murder," the *Courier* reported, "and it was this feeling, more than that of vicious curiosity, that drew together so large a crowd."

Shortly before these events occurred, residents of Hannibal had begun to feel free to actively participate in civil discussions about the issue of slavery in Missouri. Sometimes heated, debates would occasionally crop up between three different factions: proslavery advocates, abolitionists who insisted on full emancipation of the slaves and groups such as the Marion County Colonization Society, which believed that free people of African descent should be returned to Africa (other colonists around the country suggested that freed blacks should be relegated to Haiti in the Caribbean). As it became more acceptable in polite society to speak of the issues of slavery, even members of the clergy, both those who were proslavery and those who were against it, would lecture from the pulpit in an attempt to persuade their congregations.

However, after having been exposed to murder, uprising and execution, the fear that gripped Hannibal residents had an unexpected outcome: to prevent possible provocation of the slaves, all discussions over the issue of slavery were dropped. Slaves were now seen as dangerous, and to protect innocent townsfolk, particularly women and children, the rule of law must be upheld. Slavery was legal in Missouri, and it was thought best to assume the status quo and no longer discuss any other possibilities. Idle talk of emancipation or colonization, it was believed, might have serious consequences. The debate over slavery ceased, and the topic was no longer brought up. The silence was deafening.

Joseph S. Buchanan, who had begun to publish the *Pacific Monitor* back in 1840, had steered his newspaper through several incarnations and, by 1848, had renamed the paper yet again, now calling it the *Hannibal Journal*. The *Journal* by that time had become the *Missouri Courier*'s main rival for readership in Hannibal. For many years Buchanan had been a moderate antislavery advocate who supported both emancipation and colonization and had published editorials in the *Journal* exploring both of these options. Prior to the murder of the Bright children, these editorials would be fodder for healthy debate around town but would not have been considered inflammatory or morally offensive.

However, sentiments in Hannibal took a drastic turn after that fateful Halloween morning when the Bright children's bodies were discovered in the woods under the walnut trees. While no public proclamations were made, it was clear that townsfolk no longer wanted to discuss the issue of slavery. Unfortunately for Buchanan, he didn't read the signals and was unaware of the change in climate amongst his readership.

The day after Ben was arrested for the murders, Buchanan's *Journal* featured the first of seven installments on a new series discussing the issue of slavery. The essays were written under the pseudonym "Toss" and appeared in the *Hannibal Journal* between November 1 and December 13, 1849.

The "Toss Letters," as they came to be known, referred to slavery as a "curse," explaining that slavery was sinful and against the will of God. Citing Scripture, the letters expounded on the notion that the conduct of the Israelites toward their slaves in the Old Testament was not moral and should not be considered acceptable in modern times. Toss wrote that slaves were being denied their natural rights as described in the Declaration of Independence, that Christianity ended the practice of slavery in ancient Rome and therefore Christians should renounce slavery in America and that slaveholders, in effect, were in possession of stolen property that should be returned to Africa.

Immediately, there was public outcry over the "Toss Letters." Toss's incendiary arguments, it was said, would surely spread to the slave community and cause the slaves to rise up in rebellion, believing that God was on their side and that He would sustain them in their righteous quest for freedom.

Buchanan did not anticipate the furor the essays would cause. Once he realized the damage that had been done, he quickly scrambled to maintain his readership, posting the following notice in the *Journal* on December 20, 1849:

> *For several weeks past, we have been publishing a series of articles on the subject of slavery, written by "Toss," a correspondent, and was not aware that it was so strongly tinctured with abolitionism, until some of our worthy patrons made complaint...We must admit that our correspondent has shamefully imposed on us—and can say to those who have formed a wrong impression in relation to our sentiments on the slavery question, that we look to higher aim and a nobler design, than to take sides or tamper with Abolitionism, Free Soilism, Abby Kellyism, Disunionism, or any of the disgusting, contaminationisms of the day. Our readers can be assured, that hereafter we will be more particular about communications, and no such fanciful trash can again be admitted into the columns of the "Journal."*

Even after this public apology, less than a month after publishing the "Toss Letters," Buchanan's *Journal* would cease to exist, its readership and advertisers having withdrawn their support. Just one week after the hanging of Glascock's slave, Ben, in late January 1850, Buchanan offered the *Journal* office for sale and advertised that his house and lots in Hannibal were now being sold "dog cheap."

With the end of the *Hannibal Journal* also came the end of any public discussion or debate regarding the issue of slavery. Throughout the 1850s, Hannibal newspapers, including those that employed both Orion and Samuel Clemens, would continue to publish articles about slaves that, by today's standards, would be considered racist and immoral: crude jokes depicting slaves as unintelligent or childlike, articles reminding readers that slaves were dangerous and unpredictable and stories that portrayed slaves as savage, sexual animals that must be kept tame. Reflecting the sentiments of the majority of Hannibalians, the publishers furthered the ideals of proslavery advocates with their stereotypical depictions of slaves and no longer discussed in print the possibility of emancipation or colonization. These topics would not appear again in a Hannibal publication until the onset of the Civil War.

HANNIBAL'S FORTY-NINERS

On January 24, 1848, James Wilson Marshall, originally from Platte County, Missouri, stumbled across gold nuggets in the water of his sawmill near the confluence of the American and Sacramento Rivers in California. Employees of the sawmill and adjacent businesses quickly began to search the area and also discovered gold. Soon, word spread throughout California and the Oregon Territories—and thus, the California Gold Rush had begun.

It took quite a while for the news to arrive on the shores of Hannibal. When the discovery of gold in California was first reported, some Hannibalians were skeptical of what seemed like a "get-rich-quick" scheme. However, when President James Polk spoke of the discovery in his message to Congress in December 1848, people all over the United States began to dream of the riches that were waiting for them in California. Gold rush fever began to grip the town of Hannibal.

Travel from Missouri to the golden lands of California, especially in the harsh winter months of January and February, would be treacherous. Plans were made by some to travel by oxcart or horseback in April; others booked passage on clipper ships that would travel south all the way to the southern tip of South America and round Cape Horn before turning toward the western shores of North America (a voyage of more than fifteen thousand miles that could take up to eight months). A third route, one that would take less time and could commence before spring, was to cross the Isthmus of Panama. From Hannibal, one could take a steamboat south to New Orleans, catch a ship going farther south to the Central American port of Chagres, travel twenty-one miles by foot or mule across Panama and then board another ship heading north to the California border. Of course, in 1849, there were no railways heading west, and the Panama Canal wouldn't be completed until 1914.

Buchanan's *Hannibal Journal* fueled potential gold miners' gold rush fever. On December 7, 1848, the *Journal* reported that a small group of Missouri men had returned to St. Joseph from California with a large quantity of gold dust, and a local Hannibal jeweler had obtained two samples of the gold dust for locals to examine. An editorial published on December 29, 1848, spoke of "Gold Fever." One week later, on January 4, the *Journal* quoted a man from St. Louis who claimed to have made the trip from California back to Independence, Missouri, in only one hundred days by oxcart. Tilden Selmes, a merchant whose warehouse was located on the northeast corner of Main and Hill Streets, began a series of advertisements in the *Journal* proclaiming, "Ho! For California!" that offered supplies for the adventure. Gold rushers from the east began arriving in Hannibal by steamboat, stopping to gather supplies on their way west to St. Joseph and beyond. Their enthusiasm whipped some local residents into a frenzy of excitement, and the town was abuzz with reports of men banding together preparing for their trip.

The first group to set out from Hannibal for the riches of California departed on February 7, 1849. The quartet included George Wiley, attorneys A. Cook Campbell and Thomas Sunderland and Sunderland's younger brother. The four left Hannibal on a steamship bound for New Orleans in an attempt to make the trek across Panama. Sunderland sent letters back to Hannibal during his trip and described the overcrowding and disease they had to endure on their journey. The four were stranded in Panama while Sunderland's brother recovered from a bout of malaria. When they did finally make it to the Pacific shores of California, they faced swollen river streams that made panning for gold more difficult than originally thought. Further, by the time they reached their destination, the cost of living in the mining camps had been inflated by merchants taking advantage of the fortune seekers. Eventually, Sunderland would begin to practice law in Sacramento, earning badly needed revenue to sustain their mining endeavor. Many who traveled west in the gold rush found that they required employment or a secondary source of income to survive as they continued their quest for gold.

The California Gold Rush saw the territory of California grow from five hundred inhabitants in 1845 to fifty-three thousand in 1849. Just three years after becoming the thirty-first state in the Union on September 9, 1850, California's population would grow to more than a half million. Between 1848 and 1883, more than $1.2 billion in California gold was discovered.

In 1849, a total of eighty Hannibal men departed for their grand adventure west. Over the next three years, more than three hundred would make the journey. Some died en route on cholera-laden clipper ships. Others died after reaching California while living in overcrowded and unsanitary mining camps. Those traveling cross-country, such as Captain Archibald S. RoBards and his "mess" of Hannibal men (so called because they would eat as a group in a "mess tent"), reported encounters with Native Americans who were not always friendly. Charles Brady, the son of

Hannibal's first mayor, would strike it rich in the gold mines of California, but many did not. A fair number of Hannibalians settled in California and never returned to Missouri.

L<small>EAVING THE</small> N<small>EST</small>

In June 1853, Sam Clemens, now seventeen, left Hannibal to seek his fortune. Little did he know, as he stepped off the shore of the Hannibal levee onto the steamboat that would carry him away, that a grand adventure awaited him. Throughout his life he traveled the world and wrote of his experiences, yet it was Hannibal that Mark Twain thought of as his hometown, Hannibal that he remembered so vividly when he wrote *Tom Sawyer* and *Huckleberry Finn*. It was Hannibal that provided the texture to the tales he would so famously weave in his lifetime. Twain would recall time and again his childhood memories of his boyhood in Hannibal, both happy and bittersweet, in both his writings and his storytelling lectures. Hannibal's favorite son would emerge a comic genius, with humor and wit that would eventually lead him to fame and fortune. Now, more than 100 years after his death and 150 years after leaving Hannibal, Mark Twain's legacy lives on, and he is as revered and as popular as ever.

RAILROADS, WAR AND RECONSTRUCTION

Hannibal & St. Joseph Railroad

While the steamboat trade would continue to benefit cities like Hannibal for decades, the growth of railroad transport dominated the second half of the 1800s, as larger masses of people migrated to the west in search of land and riches. By the end of the 1840s, the eastern portion of the United States would already be dotted with nine thousand miles of railways, but many of the individual routes were not interconnected and did not provide service west of the Mississippi River. Whichever town could serve as an entry point to provide transportation for the westward movement would establish itself as a center of trade and manufacturing for years to come, especially if that town were to be the first to connect the territories to the more established states. Hannibal town leaders initiated a drive for such a railroad, one that would prove to be a historic and controversial achievement and would take thirteen years to plan and complete.

The Hannibal & St. Joseph Railroad (H&SJ) began at a meeting in Justice Clemens's office in the spring of 1846, as mentioned earlier, but the plan needed more than local support in order to be chartered by the state legislature. Robert M. Stewart, a state senator from St. Joseph, had been thinking along the same lines and wanted to ensure that any proposed railroad across Missouri would have St. Joseph as the terminus for the line. Stewart's political connections strongly aided the ability of the railroad group to receive a charter from the state by 1847, but not without a compromise to another state senator from Palmyra. The compromise proposed that the line that started in Hannibal would have to veer twelve miles northwest to Palmyra before heading due west across the state. Otherwise, officials from Palmyra would attempt to fund their own railroad to the Mississippi through the now-extinct village of Marion City and block state funding to the H&SJ Railroad. Another eventual compromise to ensure that Hannibal would serve as the eastern terminal was to support the construction of a thirteen-plus-mile track extending from West Quincy, Illinois, to Palmyra but running eight-tenths of a mile short of connecting with the H&SJ line. This last point was critical in preventing Hannibal from being completely bypassed as a commerce and transport center.

In return, Stewart was able to coax $100,000 in railroad subscriptions (investments) from Marion County officials and businessmen, in addition to a further $50,000 raised in Hannibal. While in retrospect the allure of a railroad line would surely have attracted investors all along the railroad's proposed path, very few people lived between Hannibal and St. Joseph to be investors. The line would be necessary to develop business along northern Missouri, but it *needed* business trade to support its route—a proverbial chicken-or-egg scenario. Nevertheless, the railroad company had gathered enough funds (including some from Stewart's own pocketbook) to begin surveying a route westward from Hannibal in 1849.

The company also needed help from the federal government in securing the land for the railroad; without it, the railroad could not afford to raise enough money to cover the construction and early operation of the line. Yet the idea of land grants to railroad companies had not established itself by 1850, when Stewart, local and railroad attorney R.F. Lakenan and Missouri representatives of the U.S. Congress lobbied the federal government for such a grant. The argument for a land grant centered on a precedent of similar grants given for the construction of overland roads and canals—roughly 3.5 million acres of land had been already given for various projects.

Though a bill granting land to the H&SJ Railroad had passed the Senate, it failed to gain traction in the House of Representatives. At the same time, Illinois politicians such as Senator Stephen A. Douglas were lobbying for a similar grant for the north–south Illinois Central line; Douglas lobbied for the House to pass the bill, underlining the difference in political clout between Illinois and Missouri at the time. The Illinois Central grant did at least enable a precedent to be set for the H&SJ that would be useful when the company reapproached Congress for help.

In the meantime, company officials believed that pervasive attempts to privately finance its early stages would convince the federal government to grant the needed amount of land to build the entire 206-mile length of track. The H&SJ company completed its survey of the eastern end of the line by the fall of 1851, and on November 3, it conducted a groundbreaking ceremony in Hannibal, replete with processionals and cannon firings. By December, a survey of the western end extending from St. Joseph had commenced.

Financially, progress had maintained a steady crawl until Congress approved a 600,000-acre land grant in 1852. The grant resembled a checkerboard pattern of plats extending six miles on either side of the proposed track. The federal government would place the even-numbered plats in state government custody, to be transferred to the company upon completion of the line. Alternate, odd-numbered plats would be retained by the federal government and not placed back on the open market until the beginning of 1855, in an effort to prevent a monopoly of land ownership and new town speculation being given to any one entity.

The land grant spurred the company to begin construction at the Hannibal end of the line in earnest. General contractor John Duff (of Duff and Leamon in New York) had won the contract to build the line in August 1852, though the original route was changed and the contract renegotiated in March 1853. Duff, sensing the needs of the company to acquire funds immediately, offered to build the line on a budget of $23,000 per mile in exchange for $1 million worth of railroad stock. In addition, Duff would retain rights to use finished portions of the railroad for his commercial benefit until the entire line was completed. Duff sold his stock to a group of Boston investors led by John Murray Forbes in late 1854, while the company sought what would eventually inflate to $3 million worth of state government–backed bonds (treated like a lien on mortgaging the land that the company would eventually receive). Beginning in early 1854 and continuing into mid-1855, construction on the line was suspended due to undercapitalization, a continuing problem not resolved until the money markets loosened and the government bonds were finally made available in 1856.

After gaining the largest piece of company ownership at the time, Forbes had found his link to the west from his other holdings, the Central Michigan and Chicago, Burlington & Quincy (CB&Q) Railroads. The fact that the

RICH FARMS AND GOOD HOMES!

AT LOW PRICES AND ON LIBERAL TERMS!

IN NORTH MISSOURI.

THE HANNIBAL & ST. JOSEPH RAILROAD COMPANY

OFFER FOR SALE OVER

400,000 ACRES

OF THE

Best Prairie, Timber and Coal Lands in the West!

IN FORTY ACRE LOTS OR MORE,

ON TWO OR TEN YEARS CREDIT!

AT PRICES RANGING FROM

$2,40 to $3, $4, $5, $6, $9, $12, $15, &c.,

AVERAGING UNDER $10 PER ACRE.

20 per Cent. is Deducted from 10 Years Credit Price if fully paid in 2 Years!

FREE FARE.—Exploring Land buyers should get tickets at Land office in Hannibal, in order to have fare on this Railroad refunded or allowed on first payment for land.

Town lots in towns on the Railroad are sold for one-third of value down, one-third in one year, and one-third in two years with interest.

These Railroad Lands are located in twenty counties in North Missouri, about as follows:

COUNTIES.	ACRES.	COUNTIES.	ACRES.
Pike	1,520	Linn	56,200
Ralls	1,560	Carroll	18,560
Marion	1,530	Livingston	60,400
Lewis	640	Grundy	4,560
Knox	280	Caldwell	62,360
Monroe	8,005	Daviess	19,080
Shelby	18,000	Clinton	89,720
Randolph	4,960	DeKalb	55,880
Macon	83,240	Buchanan	1,240
Chariton	21,550	Andrew	2,890

Hannibal and St. Joseph R. R. Land Circulars,

Giving full particulars, are furnished gratis, and persons wishing to enlist their friends to emigrate with them should apply for all they want to circulate.

A SECTIONAL MAP, showing the exact location of the lands, is sold at thirty cents. Apply by letter or otherwise to

GEO. S. HARRIS,

Land Commissioner H. & St. J. R. R.,

HANNIBAL, MO.

A handbill advertising H&SJ land for sale. Government land grants enabled the railroad to raise funds for building and operational expenses. *Courtesy Hannibal Arts Council/Fran Hafner.*

controlling interest of the H&SJ Railroad was in the East Coast (and a Union supporter during the Civil War) was mitigated by the retention of Stewart as the president of the company. Forbes stabilized the enterprise and attracted other, smaller investors merely due to his involvement. By the fall of 1856, the first twenty-five miles extending westward from Hannibal had begun operation.

At this point, it became clear that the company's contract through John Duff was one-sided, to be polite. The contract's terms encouraged him to build the line as cheaply as possible so as to pocket the remainder of the budget. Moreover, because he would maintain sole rights of the built portions until the line was completed, it behooved him to work slowly and keep the construction perpetually "in progress." As Forbes had said after the railroad was complete, "For a while the enterprise resolved itself into a contest between him and me, he wishing to build a cheap contractor's railroad to sell, and I a solid one adapted to being held and being used for business purposes." By the spring of 1857, Forbes had visited the railroad and threatened to withdraw his funding unless the contract with Duff was changed. Duff was convinced to agree on a four-month limit on operational rights for each twenty-five-mile section of track completed.

At first, even with the financial panic of 1857 looming, construction of the railroad had finally "picked up steam," with seventy-five miles of track stretching westward from Hannibal and the first ten miles eastward of St. Joseph completed. This did not mean that the conflicts with Duff had ended. He had refused to honor the portion of his renegotiated contract that called for him to relinquish control of finished track four months after construction. When the company moved to take control of the finished track, Duff and his workers impounded all locomotives and held the roundhouse as their "miniature fortress." In what was later named the "Hannibal War," the company eventually forced Duff and his men to surrender the property, but not before one man was killed in the fight. Duff had finally lost operational control, but not before siphoning $1 million in profits that would have been realized by the company under the 1857 terms of the contract.

Ironically, the company entered another contract with Duff later that year, paying him a salary of $10,000 per year to supervise subcontractors as an employee of the company until the line was finished. He possessed more knowledge of the subcontractors and their work than did the company executives; he also maintained a sizable financial stake in the Missouri

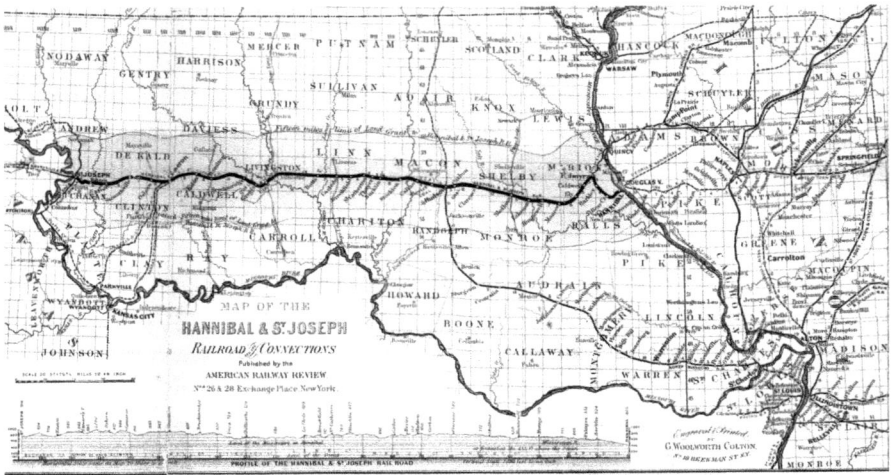

An 1860 map detailing the finished Hannibal & St. Joseph Railroad line. *Courtesy Library of Congress.*

Land Company, a shell company created by the railroad to purchase public domain land along the line that could not be bought outright.

The final spike connecting Hannibal to St. Joseph was struck at Chillicothe on February 13, 1859, almost thirteen years after the first meeting in Justice Clemens's office and over seven years after the first groundbreaking ceremony. By then, business speculation in Hannibal had set the foundation for the most successful period in the town's history, nearly tripling its population in ten years and making it the third largest city in the state, behind St. Joseph and St. Louis—all three being the first rail centers west of the Mississippi River.

Emphasis on the importance of the railroad's existence could not be overstated. First, the route was the first to cross the state of Missouri and connect to an in-progress Atchison, Topeka & Santa Fe Railroad to the west. Second, it connected the Mississippi and Missouri Rivers, offering a faster route than river traffic for passengers and some cargo. Third, eventual cooperation with the CB&Q positioned Hannibal as a pivot point for multiple railroads in the future to add service between Chicago, eastern Iowa and St. Louis. Eventually, six different lines would simultaneously provide service to and from Hannibal.

Before any of the above could happen, the railroad would have to be certified by the State of Missouri and the land grant released to

No. 5.

RAILROAD TIME CARD.
HANNIBAL, - MO.

Trains will Arrive and Depart as follows: Hannibal Union Depot Clock Time.

Depart.	CHICAGO, BURLINGTON AND QUINCY RAILROAD.	Arrive.
No. 206 Mail, daily except Sunday.	5.50 am	No. 203 Mail, except Sunday............. 9.55 am
No. 204 Chicago Express, except Sunday 5.05 pm		No. 201 Chicago Express, except Sunday 11.35 pm

HANNIBAL AND ST. JOSEPH RAILROAD.

No. 1 New York & Kansas City, daily...10.30 am	No. 4 New York & Kan. City Ex., daily. 4.00 am
No. 3 Pacific, daily.....................10.45 pm	No 2 Atlantic Express, daily.......... 4.35 pm
No. 7 Accommodation, except Sunday... 6.10 am	No. 10 Accommodation, except Sunday... 9.00 am
No. 13 Accommodation, except Sunday... 5.00 pm	No. 12 Accommodation, except Sunday... 1.20 pm

MISSOURI PACIFIC RAILWAY.

No. 151 Texas Express, daily............11.17 am	No. 154 Texas Express, daily............ 5.12 am
No. 153 Texas Express, daily............10 37 pm	No. 152 Texas Express daily............ 5.05 pm
No. 197 Wabash, except Monday. 2.02 am	Cannon Ball.	No. 198 Wabash, except Sunday. 1.22 am

ST. LOUIS, KEOKUK AND NORTHWESTERN RAILWAY.

No. 2 Mail & Exp., except Sun. 3.10 pm	Trains North	No. 1 Mail & Exp., except Sun.12.25 pm
No. 4 St Louis Express daily.. 2.25 am		No. 3 St Louis Express, daily..11.10 pm
No. 1 Mail & Exp., except Sun..12.45 pm	Trains South	No. 2 Mail & Exp., except Sun. 3.05 pm
No. 3 St. Louis Express, daily..11.20 pm		No. 4 St. Louis Exp., daily..... 2.20 am

ST. LOUIS, HANNIBAL AND KEOKUK RAILROAD.

No. 1 Mail and Express, except Sun...... 7 50 am	No. 2 Mail and Express, except Sun...... 6.45 pm
No. 3 Troy Accommodation, except Sun...7.30 pm	No. 4 Troy Accommodation, except Sun..11.00 am

WABASH, ST. LOUIS AND PACIFIC RAILWAY.

No. 94 Fast Line, except Sunday........ 5 35 am	No. 93 Fast Line, daily.................10.50 am
No. 92 Mail and Express, daily......... 5.10 pm	No. 95 Pacific Express, except Sunday..10.15 am
No. 96 Thro. Ex., except Sun... 1.30 am	Cannon Ball.	No. 91 Thro. Ex., except Mon... 1.45 am

A Hannibal time card detailing the six major railroads offering daily service, before time zone standardization (see upper right). *Courtesy Steve Chou.*

the company. Luckily for the company, R.M. Stewart had resigned his presidency after winning election as Missouri governor in 1857. Despite a conspicuous conflict of interest that prompted the legislature to make attempts to curtail his authority, Stewart certified the line in two stages. Part of the reason may have been to appear as if caution were being taken in approving the work, but another reason was that portions of the track were unballasted and other areas of the road were in poor condition. A new railroad already needed repairs.

For the railroad to earn certification, the line's investment group hired nearly one thousand laborers to repair or strengthen rail beds, tracks, switches, etc., requiring a refinancing of government bonds for the available funds. In all, the cost of the Hannibal & St. Joseph Railroad would top $12 million, over $58,000 per mile—two and a half times the original estimate! Because the cost per mile had exceeded that of other railroad systems by tens of thousands of dollars, newspapers across the state would receive letters claiming that the state had been defrauded of its bond money.

Despite the controversy surrounding the finances of its construction and its rough features, the railroad experienced instant success simply by virtue of its geography and timing. Just over a year after service from Hannibal to St. Joseph commenced, the Pony Express transcontinental mail service began running its two-thousand-mile route from St. Joseph to San Francisco, California. At the time, April 1860, the best means of delivering westbound mail to the St. Joseph office remained the H&SJ line; Hannibal had become a de facto eastern hub for the Pony Express until the latter's demise at the hands of the Union Pacific telegraph line. Until other rail lines started to crisscross Minnesota, Iowa and Missouri, the H&SJ featured prominently in the delivery of mail to lesser-developed western territories and states.

The mail trade, where transportation contracts with the federal government provided a source of consistent income for a railroad, placed a premium on efficiency: the services that could provide the fastest and most organized form of delivery to other posts would make that railroad more attractive for additional contracts. The H&SJ had already established a record speed at the time (over forty miles per hour in 1859), and on July 28, 1862, the first railway mail car built and operated in the United States rolled out from the Hannibal roundhouse.

The idea of sorting mail on a train was proposed by William A. Davis, assistant postmaster at St. Joseph. Due to repeated disruptions of train service caused mainly by sabotage from Confederate-sympathizing bushwhackers, the backlog of mail that arrived at the St. Joseph station could not be sorted fast enough to accommodate overland wagon routes to the west. If the mail were sorted during its transport, the overland delivery process time would be slashed by fourteen hours (at least one transit day). General postmaster Montgomery Blair (brother of Missouri congressman General Francis P. Blair, a close friend of Davis) authorized the construction of two thirty-foot postal cars in Quincy, Illinois, for a trial run in early July. The Quincy branch of the railroad did not meet deadlines, so officials turned to master car builder H.C. Whiting at the Hannibal maintenance shops for help.

The Hannibal crew converted a baggage car for mail use by installing sorting tables and shelving to imitate the workspace of a post office on wheels—with one exception. According to Addison Clark, engineer of the locomotive Missouri, which drove the first mail car:

The first dedicated mail rail car in the United States was created for the H&SJ Railroad. *Courtesy Hannibal Free Public Library.*

The track…was very rough and the cars, being short, got off the tracks quite often. Mr. H.W. Farley, the master mechanic, put two iron rods along the top of the car for the postal clerks to hang onto while the car was off the track, and it proved to be an excellent safety appliance.

Hannibal would continue to be the prime mover of mail across the Midwest until the completion of the Union Pacific railroad system caused a permanent shift of main postal traffic to the north.

THE RAILROAD AS CIVIL WAR FRONTLINE IN A BORDER STATE

As the H&SJ Railroad dominated in its early years as a prime mover of men and materials between the East and West, it was a vital asset to the Union and a major target of siege from the Confederacy. Missouri's status as one of four border states (states allowing slavery but not seceding from the Union) only added to its reputation as being "up for grabs."

Although Hannibal resided within the margins of Little Dixie, a previously dominant Southern and proslavery culture had been infiltrated by other influences, thanks to economic development sparked by the railroad. The largest shareholders of the H&SJ Railroad were Boston-based Unionists; in addition, the construction and trade industries required workers, a need that German and Irish-born immigrants were able to oblige. The influx of immigrants and Northern businessmen introduced another form of culture at odds with that of the original influence from the South, especially in terms of slavery. Moreover, the Federal grants provided to the railroad company for the line's construction had come with conditions, one of them being the right to transport Federal (Union) troops without restriction.

Despite appearances, Missouri's political divides were not restricted to anti- and proslavery factions. The 1860 presidential election results would show that Abraham Lincoln received only 10 percent of the state's popular vote—even less in Marion County—yet nearly every Marion County vote for Lincoln originated from Hannibal. The election featured four candidates from the Republican (Lincoln), Northern Democrat (Stephen A. Douglas), Southern Democrat (John Breckenridge, sitting vice president) and Union Constitutionalist (John Bell) Parties. None of these parties campaigned directly on the eradication of slavery but rather on future growth of slavery and other issues that would affect the economic fortune of the South. Only Breckenridge's platform threatened the secession of slaveholding states from the Union if states' rights were not respected; thus, the fact that he finished third in voting across much of the state indicated that proslavery forces were not necessarily pro-secession and that a number of voters were pro-Union but ambivalent on the issue of slavery.

Hannibal's political landscape differed from the rest of Marion County and Little Dixie because of its business interests. For the city to maintain its growth, the railroad was essential, and cutting ties with the Union meant also losing access to Northern investment, raw materials and markets, all of which had defined and supported the city's success. Even slaveholders understood the ramifications of this choice, since the local economy did not function in a way that would simply blend in with the South if secession occurred. Businessmen faced possible choices of voting with the heart, the mind *or* the pocketbook.

Taken in 1859–60, this photo showing North Main Street heading north from Bird offers the earliest view of the business district. *Courtesy Steve Chou.*

Divided loyalties within the city created unrest and suspicion. After the 1860 elections, the *Hannibal Daily Evening News*, a Southern-sympathizing paper, was formed and pulled no punches in its editorial policy. In an age before the secret ballot became law, the editor published on January 14, 1861:

A List of Republicans, Black Republicans, and Abolitionists (revised and published again by request)

The following is a list of the names of the men who voted for Lincoln in this city and county at the late presidential election. We have classified them under three different heads, so far as we have been able to learn their true position. All those marked with a *, we consider respectable and law-abiding citizens, and who would not be guilty of doing anything unbecoming gentlemen and law-abiding citizens. Those marked with a † we believe to be one degree less than an Abolitionist, while those marked with a ‡ are considered Abolitionists in the true sense of the word. Those not marked, are persons generally unknown.

The following is an example of an entry from the *Daily Evening News* list: "‡ W.E. DOANE, the man who says a Nigger is justifyable [*sic*] in taking the life of his master to obtain his freedom!—Left the city this morning."

In addition to calls from both Federal and Confederate governments for volunteer militia, local residents formed their own groups to defend their interests if attacked, some of which were initially kept secret in order not to harm the participants' businesses. Though a few sites in Missouri experienced full-fledged battles in the early stages of the Civil War, the state was riddled more with conflicts considered skirmishes—sixteen hundred of them during the length of the war, according to some historians. In addition, innumerable incidents occurred where Union forces, Confederate soldiers or Confederate-supporting bushwhackers would attack, rob, violate or humiliate unarmed citizens.

Bushwhackers were blamed for early attacks on trains running along the H&SJ Railroad through the spring and summer of 1861, firing blindly into cars suspected of carrying Federal troops, even when the cars were mainly filled with civilian passengers. In addition, bushwhackers and volunteer Confederate troops were encouraged to sabotage the railways themselves. Tracks were taken apart or rail beds damaged, and base supports of trestle bridges were cut or burned surreptitiously. In the latter instance, a train would be driven onto the bridge before an engineer realized that it had been compromised. On September 3, the sabotage culminated with a westbound train driving off a collapsing Platte Bridge outside Kansas City, killing twenty and injuring over one hundred people.

Business and consumer confidence plummeted, and railroad superintendent J.T.K. Hayward (staunch Unionist) sent dispatches to Forbes detailing his struggles with maintaining train service and giving warning about Union troops, whose actions risked turning the citizens of Hannibal against the government. On his own initiative, Hayward worked with residents along the main train route in gathering information about potential attacks; he would send his own men to shut down any potential destruction to the railroad. By the end of the year, Federal troops had established patrol points along the entire track. In 1862, Hayward and his railroad workers were absorbed directly into the military as part of the Thirty-eighth Regiment, though the men were seldom involved in actual combat. Even as skirmishes along the railroad gradually stabilized, passenger trains would run only in daylight hours during the war. Although

A Civil War drawing of a Federal encampment in Hannibal. *Courtesy Steve Chou.*

it required refinancing of its bonds to make interest payments, the only major railroad to avoid receivership during the war was the H&SJ.

The city of Hannibal mirrored the state of the railroad in that it maintained an uneasy balance between order and a siege mentality among its residents. Union forces occupied integral buildings to ensure that daily business continued apace, and prominent Southern sympathizers were watched with a close eye. At the same time, runaway slaves found by Federal troops were returned to their masters, even after the Emancipation Proclamation of 1863 (the border state would not officially approve emancipation until January 1865). Union control of the state took precedence over resolving slavery status until the outcome of the war became more obvious.

As a final note to the contradictions that enveloped Hannibal in the Civil War, Union troops would not act as emancipators but would recruit freed black men to fight for the government by mid-1863. Several freed men registered for the Massachusetts Fifty-fifth Volunteer Regiment, a sister regiment to the Fifty-fourth, which sent the first predominantly African American divisions into battle (commemorated in the 1989 film *Glory*).

Three of these men were laid to rest at Old Baptist Cemetery with other veterans of the Civil War; the cemetery (begun in the late 1830s but not incorporated until 1844) is located at the corner of Summer and Section Streets, northwest of downtown Hannibal.

LUMBER BARONS AND HANNIBAL'S GILDED AGE

Despite the Civil War and the occasional financial panic, Hannibal experienced a prolonged period of economic success throughout the second half of the 1800s that ushered in what could be considered its Gilded Age (a phrase coined by Mark Twain in his 1873 book *The Gilded Age: A Tale of Today*). The advent of the railroad reinforced and expanded the city's purpose as a trade and transportation center, and an industry arose that would take full advantage of this confluence of the Mississippi and the H&SJ, bringing Hannibal vast wealth in the form of the lumber trade.

Lumber mills had existed in Hannibal during its first couple of decades, but the construction of the westbound H&SJ Railroad attracted investors from other states to set up shop in the Bluff City. In the mid-1800s, the abundant white pine forests of Wisconsin and Minnesota supplied millions of feet of timber each year. Lumber companies in these areas would lash together their cut logs into enormous rafts—some as large as sixty-four by twelve hundred feet in size—and float their stock down the river to Hannibal. It was found to be much less expensive to finish the milled lumber in Hannibal, at the point where it would be shipped to market, rather than mill the lumber near the forests. Immense profits waited for those companies that could provide finished lumber to the South during Reconstruction and to the West as migration spread in that direction; with the river and the railroads, lumber could be sent in either direction directly from Hannibal.

By the end of the Civil War, six major lumber firms had been established, and their success spawned many imitators. In its heyday of the 1870s and '80s, the lumber business produced more than 200 million linear feet of finished lumber per year. This did not include another dozen smaller firms providing sash, door and window products. Hannibal grew to over eleven thousand residents in the late 1870s and rose to become the fourth largest manufacturer of finished lumber in the country.

Example of a lumber raft used to transport raw timber from the white pine forests to the Hannibal mills. *Courtesy Steve Chou.*

Besides processing board lumber, local mills like the J.M. Patton Mill on Lyon Street would also provide trim work, doors and sashes. *Courtesy Hannibal Arts Council.*

75

The big business of lumber was also reflected in the proliferation of downtown buildings, majestic churches and expansive homes, especially along Fifth Street, which became known as "Millionaires' Row." The following are a few of the "lumber barons," industrialists whose legacies have had a great and lasting impact on the city of Hannibal:

JOHN J. CRUIKSHANK JR.: John J. Cruikshank Sr., a Scottish immigrant, established the family's lumber business first in Galena, Illinois, and later at Alton, Illinois. In 1856, Cruikshank moved his growing business to Hannibal and handed the reins to his son, John J. Jr., in 1864. "J.J." (as John J. Jr. was often called) boosted the trade to amazing heights, averaging 40 million linear feet of lumber production per year through the 1880s.

J.J. married Annie Louise Hart (a woman twenty-six years his junior) in 1886, after a scandalous divorce from his first wife, Mary. Between the two marriages, J.J. had fathered seven children by 1894. When he retired from his company in 1897, the magnate had also expanded into coal and the

The Cruikshank lumberyard on Collier Street. The company was purported to sell an average of 40 million feet of board lumber per year in the 1880s. *Courtesy Steve Chou.*

window and sash industries. A highly competitive and driven individual, J.J. would continue to hold an office in the lumber company for years after his official retirement, keeping an eye on his investments, which were now being handled by his two eldest sons. He died in 1924, just short of eighty-seven years of age.

J.J. Cruikshank's first mansion was built in 1865 at the southeast corner of south Fifth and Lyon Streets (today the O'Donnell Funeral Home). In late 1900, construction was completed on a thirty-room, 13,500-square-foot Georgian revival mansion located at 1000 Bird Street. The mansion, called "Rock Cliff" by townspeople for its location on a bluff overlooking all of downtown, is now referred to as Rockcliffe. At the time of its construction, Rockcliffe was the largest single-family dwelling in Hannibal, a distinction that it retains today.

DAVID DUBACH: Born in January 1826 to parents of Swiss origin, David Dubach was raised in Madison, Indiana, and showed a self-starting initiative from an early age. Although Dubach migrated to Hannibal in 1858 to build a planing mill, lumberyard and brickyard, his educational and early work background involved architecture. Dubach's passion led him to design several of Hannibal's most impressive buildings of the late 1800s, including the Park Hotel, the first truly upscale hotel in Hannibal, located at the intersection of Fourth and Center Streets. (Sadly, the Park Hotel was destroyed by fire just after the turn of the twentieth century.)

During the Civil War, Dubach enlisted in Missouri's Thirty-eighth Regiment, assigned to protect the railroads for the Union. Other Hannibal businessmen, such as J.J. Cruikshank Jr., also enlisted, mainly to protect their business interests. After the war, Dubach added to his business portfolio by opening the Magnolia Flour Mill in 1866 and the Empire Flour Mill in 1875; he would serve as president of the latter until his death.

His wealth was well represented in town, as evidenced by the Italianate villa he built in 1871 for his family on Millionaires' Row at the southwest corner of Bird and North Fifth Streets.

In 1881, Dubach assumed the presidency of Dells Lumber Company of Eau Claire, Wisconsin, which provided the white pine for his local lumber mills. Like many of the other major lumber firms in Hannibal, Dubach's business suffered after the depletion of the northern pine forests. He sold his Hannibal lumber and brick companies in the 1890s, and Dells Lumber

The house of David Dubach shortly after its completion in 1871, at the southwest corner of North Fifth and Bird streets. *Courtesy Steve Chou.*

Company would close at the turn of the century, just three years after Dubach's death in 1897.

WILLIAM H. DULANY: A gentleman who had literally struck gold in the California Gold Rush, Dulany used his fortune to fund tobacco businesses in Paris, Missouri, and Quincy, Illinois, before joining his brother, Daniel, in the Dulany and McVeigh Lumber Company. The company, formed in 1867, eventually merged into the Empire Lumber Company, which produced as many as 28 million feet of lumber annually. Dulany's company later purchased pine forests outside the popular regions of Eau Claire, Wisconsin, and Winona, Minnesota, as well as investing in other wholesale yards up and down the Mississippi to meet demand. The Hannibal yards stretched

Cabinet card portrait of
William Dulany. *Courtesy
Hannibal Free Public Library*.

for blocks down Collier Street and occupied some thirty-nine acres until
the yard was destroyed by fire about 1895. With the forests dwindling by
that time, the company was liquidated and the land sold to the Hannibal
Businessmen's Association, a turning point in the economic redevelopment
of Hannibal as the lumber business faded.

JOHN H. GARTH: Garth is considered one of Hannibal's lumber barons, as
he served as president of the Garth Lumber Company of Delta, Michigan,
but his impact on Hannibal encompassed many other industries based in
Hannibal. His parents, John and Emily, had relocated their family to Hannibal
in 1842, when John H. was five years old; here, the senior Garth established
a large tobacco factory and grain business. John H. was a childhood friend
of Samuel Clemens, attended private school in Kentucky, enrolled in the
University of Missouri in 1851 and graduated in 1854 at the age of seventeen.
After graduation, he traveled between Hannibal and New York over the next

seventeen years with his brother, D. J. Their firm specialized in banking and brokerage services in addition to its investments in manufacturing.

Garth began construction of his mansion on Millionaires' Row at 213 South Fifth Street just after the Civil War. Completed in 1869, the mansion became his family's winter home after Garth purchased a six-hundred-acre farm three miles southwest of the city limits the following year and built a twenty-room summer residence, named Woodside, in 1871–72. Garth was one of the incorporating members of the Farmers' and Merchants' Bank, beginning as vice-president but quickly rising to the office of president. Since his tenure, the bank has been in continual operation and remains a vital part of the Hannibal community to the present day.

Before his death in 1899, John H. Garth had also served as president of the lucrative Hannibal Lime Company and the Missouri Guarantee, Savings and Building Association. He also bred specialty Jersey cattle. After his death, his wife, Helen, donated $25,000 for the creation of a memorial to her husband, the John H. Garth Memorial Library. A prime example of Beaux Arts architecture inspired by the 1893 Chicago World's Fair, the library was completed in 1902 and was the first taxpayer-funded, "free" public library in the state of Missouri.

SUMNER T. MCKNIGHT: Milwaukee native McKnight began his Hannibal lumber business in 1862, processing raw timber from Wisconsin. In 1873, his firm merged with D.R. Moon of Eau Claire, Wisconsin, and became part of the Northwestern Lumber Company. The move combined lumberyards in Eau Claire, Hannibal and St. Joseph to create a conglomerate that sold 48 million feet of lumber in 1883 (25 million from the Hannibal yards alone).

One remarkable contribution from McKnight was the design for a railroad transport car system that could dip into the river at barge level, allowing direct loading of timber from a carrier to the yards without any intermediate steps. This invention was a first in its industry, and its patent led to the formation of the Hannibal Transfer Company in early 1882. At least four large lumber firms subscribed to this service in the first year alone.

McKnight moved into his custom-built, five-thousand-square-foot Eastlake Italianate manse in 1877, situated on the bluff above Bird Street near Tenth Street. (In the late 1890s, after McKnight had relocated out of state, his home would be moved three hundred feet to the west on a log "dolly" to make room for the construction of Cruikshank's Rockcliffe Mansion.)

W.B. PETTIBONE: The Pettibone family started their lumber fortune—like many others at the time—in Wisconsin. The family fortune originated from La Crosse, where patriarch A.W. Pettibone and his business partner, G.D. Hixon, were regarded as two of the most influential men in town. The pair's self-titled lumber company was founded in Hannibal in 1867; a fire destroyed the mill in October 1882, just as the company had begun reaching 24 million feet of lumber production per year. From the ashes of Hixon and Pettibone arose the Hannibal Sawmill Company, headed by A.W. and managed by his eldest son, Wilson Boyd (W.B.) Pettibone. Due to W.B.'s business savvy, Hannibal Sawmill Company outlived most of the other lumber companies in the area.

Today, Millionaires' Row retains two monuments of the Pettibone fortune. The first was finished for W.B. and his family in 1889, a double-turreted, three-story Queen Anne at 313 North Fifth Street. The second house was built on the same block, at the corner of Fifth and Bird Streets, for younger brother A.W. Pettibone Jr. in 1895. A.W. Jr., a graduate of Yale University in 1893, died tragically of pneumonia in 1899, just twenty-nine years old. Today, both homes are beautifully preserved and serve as bed-and-breakfast inns.

W.B. Pettibone was, throughout his life, one of the most philanthropic men in Hannibal. Anonymously, he would donate funds for civic projects, including street repairs, school construction and playgrounds. He personally insured children's bank accounts during the Great Depression after banks began to fail and helped to build an orphanage.

Possibly his greatest donation to the city, however, continues to serve tens of thousands of residents and visitors each year. Pettibone donated a beautiful parcel of land, over 450 acres of prime real estate overlooking the Mississippi River, to the City of Hannibal to form what is now known as Riverview Park. He also bought parcels of land around the perimeter of the park area so that no encroachment of development would spoil the park's ambiance. Pettibone retained O.C. Simonds, a world-renowned landscape architect (and the person selected by J.J. Cruikshank to design the gardens for Rockcliffe Mansion in 1901), to plan the park's design and oversee its construction. Simonds implemented a series of winding carriage paths to lead park visitors through specially planned garden areas and to scenic points with breathtaking views of the river. Riverview Park was initiated in 1909 and today is one of the crown jewels of Hannibal. The park is a popular tourist

An early image of Riverview Park, the largest gift to the city from philanthropist lumberman W.B. Pettibone. *Courtesy Hannibal Free Public Library.*

destination and features a large statue of Mark Twain standing majestically at the precipice of a tall bluff, looking out over his beloved Mississippi River. Riverview Park is now listed on the National Register of Historic Places.

Shortly after the establishment of Riverview Park, W.B. Pettibone purchased the property at the corner of Bird and Stillwell Place, just west of the McKnight and Cruikshank mansions. Due to the deteriorating condition of the 1861 residence in place at the time, Pettibone demolished the old mansion in 1911 and hired internationally known Chicago School architect Howard Van Doren Shaw to erect a new home. The 10,500-square-foot mansion contains nineteen rooms and reflects a strong English Arts and Crafts sensibility, including a love for nature: all the gathering and entertaining rooms on the first floor possess floor-to-ceiling French doors that lead directly outside to a croquet lawn framing the view of Hannibal's southern bluffs. Pettibone lived at the mansion at 8 Stillwell Place, now known as Cliffside Mansion, until his death in 1946. The mansion was maintained within the family until 1957, when it was converted to the Shady Lawn Convalescent

Home for some thirty years. Currently, it has been restored back to a private residence that opens its doors for local special events and weddings.

AMOS J. STILLWELL: Originally born in Maysville, Kentucky, in 1828, Amos and his brother, Brison, moved to Hannibal in 1848 to begin a milling business at Bear Creek, the first of several ventures that eventually led Stillwell to become one of the wealthiest men in Marion County. He left Hannibal for St. Louis in 1851 to form the financial firm Moffit & Stillwell, only to return to Hannibal permanently in 1855. He used the funds earned from his time in St. Louis to commence a pork-processing business on Front Street. His processed Stillwell hams were so successful that Queen Victoria of England would not eat any ham other than Stillwell's brand, sending for them to be shipped overseas.

Later, Stillwell would become president of the Hannibal Lumber Company. As part of the firm Hayward, Stillwell & Co., he was responsible for completion of the first section of the Missouri, Kansas & Texas Railroad that stretched from Naples, Illinois, to Moberly, Missouri (the K-T, or "Katy," later extended south to Texas). He also served as president of the First National Bank from the Panic of 1873 to its voluntary liquidation in 1879. Stillwell's later investments included a six-hundred-acre farm and one of the largest ice/cold storage businesses in the state, where teams of horses would cut huge chunks of ice from the frozen Mississippi River to be stored and sold for summer use.

A view of Fifth Street (also known as Millionaires' Row) in the 1890s, looking north from Broadway. *Courtesy Steve Chou.*

Amos Stillwell died at the age of sixty, murdered by a blow to the head with an axe while sleeping in his mansion on Millionaires' Row. The Stillwell murder was considered the crime of the century in Hannibal, and although Stillwell's wife, Fannie, and her second husband, Joseph C. Hearne, were arrested for his murder, they were acquitted. The crime remains unsolved. The Stillwell Mansion, the scene of the crime, was demolished and replaced with the F&M Bank parking lot in 1973.

Abundant wealth was generated in Hannibal during Reconstruction and into the turn of the twentieth century. Hannibal's affluent citizens enjoyed the lavish lifestyle of the Victorian era, living in beautifully appointed mansions and traveling the world. Hannibal was considered a cosmopolitan midwestern city with sophistication and culture.

These lumber barons, along with other prominent businessmen in Hannibal, shared a sense of civic responsibility that came with their status within the community. In an era decades before the institution of income taxes, the wealthy would be called upon to help form a social safety net through their contributions, both financial and otherwise. When a Home for the Friendless (orphanage) or hospital needed to be built, businessmen would subscribe funds to support the mission and serve on oversight boards, usually without compensation. These prominent Hannibalians were brothers in fraternal organizations such as the Odd Fellows, Elks and Freemasons, board members of civic organizations and committeemen who made important decisions for the general good. Their contributions to the Hannibal community were commensurate with their wealth and business influence.

The influence of wealth was also expressed in public buildings erected during this time, grand structures designed to uplift the masses. Architecturally, buildings from this era tended to hearken back to Classical, European-influenced design. For example, the Old Jail was built in 1878 to house prisoners and the police station. The double-turreted, Byzantine-influenced structure was used by the police for ninety-nine years, and the building still exists at the corner of South Fourth and Church Streets with the original jail cells intact. The Gothic-influenced Federal Building, completed in 1888, boasted not only the post office but also the Northeast Missouri Postmaster General's Office, a U.S. Weather Bureau station and the U.S. District and Circuit Courts for Missouri's Eastern District. The building, located on Broadway between Sixth and Seventh Streets, served the government until 1960 and is now available for privately owned businesses.

Right: The nicknamed "Federal Building" was completed in 1888 due in large part to the efforts of U.S. representative William Henry Hatch. *Courtesy Hannibal Free Public Library*.

Below: A view of the tracks looking south along the riverfront. The building in the right background is the Hannibal Union Depot. *Courtesy Steve Chou*.

Roughly three blocks away, the Neoclassical, rotunda-topped Marion County Courthouse was built on Broadway at Tenth Street. Although Hannibal had never been the county seat (Palmyra, twelve miles northwest of Hannibal, served that distinction), most of the county's population lived in or near Hannibal. In those days, demands were made for a more reasonable means of conducting government business; traveling to Palmyra by horseback to file deeds drew complaints. Thus, a second county courthouse in Hannibal was erected, and it is still used today for Marion County business.

The most necessary of the grand buildings from this period, the Union Depot, was erected in 1882 and located on the east side of South Main, two blocks south of Broadway. Before its construction, Hannibal did not possess a central train station, and passengers were directed to the Kettering Hotel lobby on South Main (leased by the railroads for this purpose by then owner John J. Cruikshank Sr.). With six different railroad routes passing

An example of a roundhouse, nicknamed the "old Burlington Yards," in Hannibal, circa 1890. *Courtesy Hannibal Arts Council/Archie Hayden.*

through Hannibal at that time and passenger trade increasing, a larger, more organized location was essential for growth.

The new depot was an impressive landmark, three stories high with a central skylight and clock tower. The main feature of the first floor was a large waiting room with impressive woodwork, while a smaller waiting room was designated for ladies. The Union News Company operated a newsstand next to the concession area, and the two upper floors offered twenty-two hotel rooms for overnight travelers. It boasted modern plumbing and steam heat throughout. Union Depot would provide services for the Wabash, the Katy, the H&SJ, the CB&Q and the St. Louis, Keokuk & Northwest railway companies. In 1953, after train service was replaced by increased automobile traffic in Hannibal, the Union Depot was demolished to make room for a much smaller office space for the Burlington (later BNSF) Company.

Hannibal also remained competitive with other midwestern cities in staying at the front of the technology curve. The Wabash Bridge opened for train and other transport business in 1871, one of the earliest bridges to cross the Upper Mississippi.

The city established both the first phone service in Missouri in 1879 (beating St. Louis by only a matter of hours) and the first electric trolley (streetcar) system in the state in 1890. The latter event was made

Union Depot was built in 1882 and served five railways at once when opened. The building was demolished for a smaller Burlington station in 1952. *Courtesy Hannibal Free Public Library.*

The Wabash Bridge, completed in 1871, was designed on a swinging open-span system to allow steamboat traffic (as opposed to a drawbridge-style span, which requires the bridge to be built at a higher elevation). *Courtesy Hannibal Free Public Library.*

The first day of service for the first electric trolley in Hannibal, also the first such service in the state, August 1, 1890. *Courtesy Hannibal Free Public Library.*

possible after a $20,000 bond issue was approved in 1885 to finance the construction of a generating plant and eleven light towers distributed across the city, providing the entire downtown area with municipal electric service beginning in May 1886.

Interior of an electric trolley heading for Oakwood, a neighborhood at the southwestern end of the city. *Courtesy Hannibal Free Public Library.*

Hannibal's wealth and prosperity began to decline in the 1890s. The city suffered from a slowdown in population growth, partially as Hannibalians began to move to residential developments just outside the city limits. Fire, always a major concern in a city surrounded by acres of lumber, destroyed two blocks of buildings on South Main Street in 1893, causing further financial hardship.

While the first two setbacks were temporary, a third was more gradual and permanent. By the 1890s, railroad systems had proliferated across the midwestern states to the point that Hannibal was no longer a main western rail hub. To make matters more difficult, the white pine forests of Wisconsin and Minnesota that provided logs to the city's lumber mills were rapidly being depleted. A few large lumber firms would continue business into the twentieth century, but at a small fraction of the pace set a generation earlier. The era of the lumber barons trickled to a close; by 1901, only 7 million linear feet of lumber were produced in Hannibal, down from the high of 230 million feet produced in 1883.

Luckily, local investors saw this inevitability just in time.

NEW CENTURY, NEW INDUSTRY

Foreseeing the inevitable, Hannibal's civic leaders scrambled to overcome the economic hardship that was imminent due to the loss of the lumber industry. A group of forward-thinking businessmen had formed the Hannibal Businessmen's Association (HBA) in the 1880s, and this group became even more active in the 1890s as it attempted to attract new economic activity to the area.

A pivotal event in the regeneration of Hannibal industry arrived in 1897, as the association competed to be the new site of the "Missouri Colony for the Feeble-Minded and Epileptics," a large-scale project that would bring jobs and state funding to Hannibal. The town of Marshall eventually won the rights battle, but this loss inspired local businessmen to take a more aggressive stance in recruiting new industry. The HBA, noticing that the Empire Lumber Company was closing its doors, arranged to purchase its thirty-three acres of land from South Seventh Street westward along Collier Street. The HBA could then offer parcels of the property for free to companies as an incentive to relocate. Prospective companies were also given favorable loans for the construction of factories; often, the city paid up to half of the construction costs, receiving in return signed contracts that included guarantees from the companies to pay a certain amount of total wages spread over the life of the contract. The first company to take advantage of this arrangement was the newly formed St. Louis shoe company Roberts, Johnson and Rand, which began operating in Hannibal in 1898.

The shoe industry in Hannibal grew from humble beginnings. Henry Harrig, a cobbler operating his one-man business on the second floor of a shop on North Main Street, attracted the attention of R.L. Hixson. Harrig's operation evolved into the Hixson Shoe Company and moved to 403 Bird Street. By the beginning of 1898, thanks to a new invention that enabled shoe uppers and soles to be stitched together by machine, the prolific company was producing more shoes than the area could consume. Hixson, now president of the company, sent salesmen to pursue other markets outside Hannibal. When Hixson learned that one of his salesmen had been rejected by Roberts, Johnson and Rand, he traveled to St. Louis personally and gave a detailed and persuasive presentation to the company on how his new "Star" shoe brand would change its business. He walked away from the meeting with a contract to supply Star-brand shoes for Roberts, Johnson and Rand.

By 1904, the Roberts, Johnson and Rand Shoe Company had expanded to the point of building a second connecting factory on its site in Hannibal, home of Star Brand shoes. *Courtesy Steve Chou.*

However, Hixson soon learned that his shop would not be able to keep up with the demands for the product. By the end of 1898, Roberts, Johnson and Rand agreed to inject more capital into the company, reorganizing it into the Star Shoe Company and refashioning the board of directors to contain the main members of the parent company and members of the Hannibal Businessmen's Association. At this point, Roberts, Johnson and Rand was approached by the HBA and encouraged to build a new factory at South Seventh and Collier Streets. In return for free land and partial funding of the factory, the company committed to pay $350,000 in workers' wages within seven years.

By 1904, the commitment to pay promised wages had been fulfilled years ahead of schedule, and demand for Star-brand shoes boomed to the point that a second building was constructed on the property. Combined, the twin factories occupied an entire city block and boasted a manufacturing capacity of eight thousand pairs of shoes daily. As a whole, the Hannibal facility was considered one of the largest, if not *the* largest, shoe manufacturers in the country at the time. Roberts, Johnson and Rand took the business formula that worked in Hannibal and approached other cities in Missouri and Illinois with the same proposition that the Hannibal Businessmen's Association had used, and by 1908, the company had established a total of twelve shoe and sole manufacturing plants—all manufacturing the type of shoe pioneered in Hannibal. The Hannibal plants alone could produce one million pairs of shoes annually, just under 20 percent of what the company sold as a whole.

Roberts, Johnson and Rand was only one of a number of beneficiaries from the land offers given by the Hannibal Businessmen's Association. Another local shoemaker, John Logan Jr., had evolved his cobbling business into the Bluff City Shoe Company and received land from the HBA for construction of a factory on Collier Street in 1904. Also receiving land on Collier and a construction financing deal during this time was the Beggs-Goodson Wagon Company, which had relocated to Hannibal from Carrollton, Missouri.

By the mid-1910s, Collier Street was loaded with factories that produced everything from buttons and cleaning machines to railroad car wheels and cast-iron stoves. Due to the influx of new jobs and annexed land, Hannibal's population grew over 40 percent between 1900 and 1910, rising

Staff of Hannibal's Duffy-Trowbridge Foundry in the mid- to late 1890s. This was the largest manufacturer of cast-iron heating and cooking stoves in the Midwest, producing up to fifty-three thousand stoves per year. *Courtesy of Steve Chou.*

to 18,341 residents. The Hannibal Businessmen's Association dovetailed with another business association to form the Hannibal Commercial Club in 1909 (later renamed the Hannibal Chamber of Commerce). The club played an active role in more than just establishing new factories; it also championed the cause for a more easily navigated road between Hannibal and St. Joseph and initiated the formation of a statewide group of Missouri commercial associations.

During this time of industrial growth, two giants emerged. The first, Atlas Portland Cement Company, built what was then billed as "the largest cement plant in the world." Construction on the new cement plant was completed in 1901, with the facility located just a couple miles south of the city limits. The factory drew a large number of Hungarian, Italian, Slavic and Polish immigrants, and the settlement they formed in the shadow of the factory grew into a town named Ilasco, an acronym for components necessary to manufacture cement (iron, lime, aluminum, silica, coal and oxygen). A suburb of Ilasco, named Monkey Run, was formed to assist in housing the thousands of workers at the company's two facilities. By 1921, Ilasco

Workers in the shoe-sizing department at the Bluff City Shoe Factory, circa 1917. *Courtesy Hannibal Arts Council/Family of John Logan.*

had been converted into a "company town," where the cement company's employees worked, lived and shopped in the vicinity of the plant.

The second manufacturing giant of the Hannibal area grew more gradually. In 1911, the Roberts, Johnson and Rand Shoe Company acquired the East Coast–based Peters Shoe Company and morphed into International Shoe Company. The merger was only the first of many acquisitions that the new entity would add to its roster through the decades, expanding from coast to coast. Among the dozens of factories absorbed into the company, Bluff City Shoe Company was sold to International Shoe in 1925, and the Hannibal Rubber Plant facility nearby was purchased and converted into a sole production plant in the same year. By then, the shoe company employed a lion's share of the workers in the Hannibal area; estimates vary, but the top numbers indicate a maximum of five thousand workers among all its Hannibal plants and subsidiaries, producing 6 million pairs of shoes per year.

◆—◆

Hannibal's transformation from a nineteenth-century lumber and railroad town into a twentieth-century manufacturing center was complete. However, the growth of factory jobs did not parallel the type of financial success found in Hannibal's previous generations of local business. During this period, the larger companies' headquarters were usually in other cities, and their owners generally did not live in Hannibal; also, wages tended to be flat throughout the different plants, meaning that workers faced a slower road to upward mobility and reinvestment in the city's economy.

The idea of leisure time had changed dramatically, too. Nickelodeons and ball fields now dotted the downtown area. The Park Theatre, built on Center Street facing Central Park in 1882, started as a venue for concerts and plays but began to incorporate movie showings by 1913 (the Park Theatre was demolished in 1992). Two theaters that combined vaudeville shows with silent film showings were the Star on 212 South Main (built in 1906) and the Orpheum at the corner of Fifth and Broadway (built in 1922).

Another popular amusement came in the form of festivals. Downtown merchants began organizing the Fall Festival, which eventually morphed into the Fall Fiesta. The festivals included attractions as diverse as trapeze artists,

The cigar rolling operation at Hannibal's Red Star Cigar Shop circa 1900. *Courtesy Steve Chou.*

South Main Street, circa 1910, looking north. The Star Theater on the left (built in 1906) and the Mark Twain Hotel (built in 1905) still stand today. Note the lack of autos. *Courtesy Steve Chou.*

Arches lit at night for one of Hannibal's early fall celebrations. The view is looking west from Broadway and Main. The shadow in the center is a public water fountain for people—and horses. *Courtesy Hannibal Free Public Library.*

floral parades, carnival rides, musical performances and other novelties. Another annual celebration was the Chautauqua, a midsummer tradition from 1905 through the end of the 1920s. The Chautauqua was unique and suited to its social time frame, featuring more intellectually oriented events such as music recitals, plays, comic routines, sermons and philosophical lectures. Church revivals, which would sometimes draw thousands over the course of several days, also enjoyed popularity during the early years of the twentieth century.

As baseball emerged as a prominent form of amusement and spectatorship across the country, Hannibal, too, caught baseball fever. Minor-league and semiprofessional teams had operated sporadically since the 1880s in town, but the construction of Clemens Field on the former Cruikshank lumberyards provided a quality ballpark in 1925 that accommodated two thousand spectators. Originally located at Third and Collier Streets, the ball field's grandstand was destroyed by fire; when it was rebuilt in 1935, the grandstand was located farther west toward Fifth Street. In 2008, Clemens Field was again restored and is currently home to an independent-league team, the Hannibal Cavemen.

A HERO'S WELCOME

Perhaps symbolic of the closing of the Gilded Age, Mark Twain made his final and most well-known visit to Hannibal for four days in late May/early June 1902. Twain was on his way to Columbia, where he was being given an honorary doctorate degree from the University of Missouri. He was accompanied by a reporter from the *St. Louis Post-Dispatch*, who provided a detailed account of his hometown visit. Besides visiting and posing for photographs in front of his boyhood home on Hill Street, he attended

Mark Twain's 1902 visit to Hannibal attracted national attention to the river town. Here, Twain poses in front of his boyhood home on Hill Street. *Courtesy Hannibal Free Public Library/Anna Schnitzlein Collection.*

dinners held in his honor at the Garth and Clayton homes, visited his old schoolmate Laura Hawkins-Frazer, spoke to the 1902 graduating class of Hannibal High School, visited his family grave site at Mt. Olivet Cemetery and addressed a crowd of more than three hundred guests from the grand staircase of the Cruikshank mansion. The four-day visit marked a moment in time where the literary icon became a metaphor symbolizing the evolution of Hannibal, from its humble beginnings as a "white town drowsing" to its transformation into a cosmopolitan city whose wealth had peaked during the Gilded Age.

THE TWENTIETH CENTURY

PROHIBITION AND THE RED-LIGHT DISTRICT

The 1920s saw the dawn of a cultural revolution in America, and Hannibal became "under the influence." The genteel, Victorian days of the Gilded Age and Chautauquas gave way to a new generation, one that had suffered through World War I and was ready to seek new thrills and adventures. Young women, in particular, underwent a transformation: they won the right to vote, bobbed their hair and shortened their skirts. They embraced a new sense of personal freedom. The Roaring Twenties had arrived.

During this time, 111 Bird Street was one of the most famous, and infamous, addresses in all of Hannibal. If you needed a sip during Prohibition, 111 Bird Street was your destination. Soldiers and salesmen traveling cross-country by train passed the word that, if you were lucky enough to stop in Hannibal, Missouri, you had to visit 111 Bird. Local townsfolk knew they could relax and unwind for a few hours, and their privacy would be kept private, if they went to 111 Bird.

In 1917, Sarah Smith made her way from Chicago to the banks of the Mississippi in Hannibal. At the foot of Bird Street, where it met the riverfront at Front Street, Madam Sarah began construction on a unique building, the only one known to be specifically designed and built for its particularly special purpose—namely, the finest bordello in town. The square, brick building featured a "meet and greet" area, a speakeasy, a gambling room and ten small private rooms on the first floor; upstairs, an additional fourteen small rooms were available for private entertaining. It would always be called by its address (speaking an actual name out loud would be too scandalous).

Number 111 Bird Street was just one of many such businesses being conducted at that time in Hannibal; the area of Main Street north of Bird was known as the town's red-light district. On the east side of Main, a men's store sold hats and tobacco by day but hosted a notoriously serious card game in the store's back room every night. Speakeasies dotted Main Street on both sides but were made more public when they converted into regular taverns after the repeal of Prohibition. And, of course, there were the brothels. One such establishment, on the east side of North Main just a block away from the hat and tobacco shop, was a restaurant owned by a lady named Pauline. Her main source of income, however, was upstairs above the restaurant. Her girls would stand in front of the lace-draped windows on the second floor to advertise their services, and Pauline herself was frequently seen stepping outside to sweep the front stoop of her building wearing nothing more than her shoes.

As with most towns' red-light districts, many colorful characters would stop off at Hannibal as they traveled south to St. Louis, north to Iowa and

View from Cardiff Hill looking south along North Main, circa 1934. During this time, portions of North Main housed businesses related to Hannibal's red-light district. *Courtesy Steve Chou.*

Minnesota or west to Kansas City. Gamblers, railroad men, soldiers and traveling musicians all made their way to 111 Bird Street. Business flourished through Prohibition, the Great Depression and World War II.

Hannibalians and the city's police seemed to be rather tolerant of the establishments in the red-light district. One theory is that because all these businesses were clustered in the same area at the north end of Main Street, people knew where the line was drawn, so to speak, and the police could keep that sort of activity contained in one specific area rather than having to worry about it being scattered here and there all over town. The rowdies and good-timers were all kept under a watchful eye and were tolerated as long as they didn't interfere with the "respectable" businesses and townspeople in other areas of the city. Also, the "girls" were highly respected citizens in Hannibal. They were earning good money and would spend it with local merchants; they paid their bills on time, and they could keep secrets, many secrets—discretion being of vital importance, particularly to those clients who were local Hannibalians.

Hannibal's red-light district came to a rather abrupt end during the early 1950s. After World War II, America seemed to turn back to a more traditional sensibility, and areas of prostitution and gambling were forced to become more clandestine. In Hannibal, local ministers rallied their congregations to denounce these vices and put pressure on the police to clean up Main Street. The end of an era was at hand.

Of course, the buildings that used to house the taverns and brothels in downtown Hannibal are now ice cream parlors, antique stores and souvenir shops. Today, all that's left of the Prohibition-era speakeasies and gambling dens are the stories that were left behind.

Depression and Dillinger

When America fell into the depths of the Great Depression, Hannibal suffered as well. Banks closed, neighbors moved in together to save money and wages dropped. In 1930, a "free soup house" was set up at 309 South Main Street, and after only four months it had served 10,578 meals.

In 1935, President Roosevelt initiated the Works Progress Administration (WPA), which brought badly needed jobs and civic progress to Hannibal. WPA projects scheduled for Hannibal in the mid- to late-1930s included the paving of county roads; the construction of the fire department; the building

The interior of a grocery store in "The Wedge" during the early 1930s. The Wedge was a business district that began where Broadway and Market dovetailed and ran west along Market. *Courtesy Hannibal Free Public Library*.

of the Coontz Armory, a new high school stadium, Clemens (baseball) Field and the Hatch Experimental Farm; a new rock quarry; sewer installation; and the removal of old streetcar lines.

One industry in Hannibal was solid through the Depression years: the shoe factories. The International Shoe Company's three factories could produce twenty-four thousand pairs per day and employed more than five thousand workers. The shoes were offered at low retail prices, making them affordable to the masses.

One of the outcomes of the financial desperation people felt during the Great Depression was an increase in bank robberies. The decade of the 1930s spawned many high-profile gangsters, such as Jake the Barber, Pretty Boy Floyd and Bonnie and Clyde. Hannibal would have its own brush with one of the most celebrated robbers of the 1930s: John Dillinger.

On January 9, 1934, Dillinger and his gang were in Hannibal. They crept into the Murphy Motor Company building at 210 Center Street and jumped into an Oldsmobile. As Dillinger attempted to steal the car, Hannibal police gave chase. Headed northward on a dirt road, the police and the Dillinger

Above: The Orpheum Theatre as the backdrop for a giveaway held during the Great Depression, circa 1931. *Courtesy Steve Chou.*

Right: Hannibal police displaying the damage inflicted by John Dillinger's crew during a 1934 ambush. Standing next to the car are Police Chief William J. Schneider (left) and Lieutenant J.O. Barker. *Courtesy Steve Chou.*

gang exchanged gunfire. The police, unprepared for the situation, ran out of ammunition and had to drop their pursuit. They returned to the station.

Soon, the police were tipped off that Dillinger had been spotted at the Willard Cruser Farm. Two officers, W.J. Schneider and J.O. Barker, jumped into the police car and headed west on Highway 36. Somehow, Dillinger had anticipated their actions and ambushed the officers, riddling the police car with machine gun blasts.

The two officers huddled below the dash. Dillinger, who apparently did not want to injure the police, shot high and aimed with the intention of only hitting the upper windshield and top of the car. The police officers survived the encounter unscathed; Dillinger was not apprehended.

THE MARK TWAIN CENTENNIAL

In 1935, while still suffering through the Great Depression, Mark Twain's 100th birthday gave Hannibal a reason to celebrate. As early as 1930, a committee of representatives from Hannibal's service clubs gathered to plan the centennial. The committee decided to prepare a yearlong celebration, of which there would be two main centerpieces: a temporary Mark Twain Museum, housed in the Hannibal Trust Company building at the corner of Broadway and Third Street, and a new monument, the Mark Twain Memorial Lighthouse, perched on the bluffs of Cardiff Hill.

On November 11, 1934, construction on the lighthouse was commenced. The lighthouse, the first in the nation to be "inland" (which rendered it purely for decoration), would be built with WPA labor and dedicated by President Franklin Delano Roosevelt from the White House on January 15, 1935, to open the yearlong celebration. Technicians installed lines that connected the beacon of the lighthouse to the president's desk in the Oval Office so that he could light the beacon with the turn of a key. Radio stations across the country broadcast the dedication, which featured an address by President Roosevelt from the White House and comments from Clara Clemens Gabrilowitsch, Mark Twain's daughter, speaking from Detroit.

The Mark Twain Museum held its dedication celebration on April 26, 1935. Thousands gathered on Broadway to attend the ceremony. The Burlington Railway dedicated a special train to bring Clara Clemens Gabrilowitsch and her daughter, Nina (Twain's granddaughter), from Detroit to Hannibal. The museum would feature both loaned and permanently donated exhibits of Mark Twain collections. St. Louis artist Walter Russell donated to the museum a model of a proposed monument that featured Twain and twenty-four of his fictional characters (the monument was never commissioned; the

Circa 1935 postcard of Broadway looking west from Main Street. *Courtesy Hannibal Free Public Library.*

remarkable model is, at the time of this writing, currently on display at the Mark Twain Museum's Interpretive Center).

The centennial celebration continued throughout the year. Hannibal High School performed a Jubilee Concert. A nationwide Mark Twain essay contest was held. "Tom Sawyer Day" was held on May 10, and more than four thousand Hannibal Public School students marched in a parade. A pageant, *On the Banks Of Old Man River*, was presented by elementary school students. Another pageant, *Mark Twain's First One Hundred Years*, was presented and included more than eleven hundred people from Hannibal and neighboring towns in the cast. The Centennial Homecoming Festival was held in September, with a parade, musical concerts, a food tent and an art show.

On October 25, the Mark Twain Zephyr was presented in Hannibal as part of the centennial celebration. The Chicago, Burlington & Quincy Railroad had commissioned the stainless steel, art deco–style passenger train that was capable of reaching speeds as high as 122 miles per hour. The cars were named for characters in Mark Twain's writings: the locomotive was named Injun Joe; the sixty-four-foot-long baggage car was named Becky Thatcher; the kitchen and dining car was named Huckleberry Finn; and the Tom Sawyer car housed coach seats for forty passengers

The Mark Twain Zephyr's debut in Hannibal on October 25, 1935, as part of the Mark Twain Centennial celebration. *Courtesy Steve Chou/Frazier Photo.*

in the fore section, while a solarium parlor lounge for sixteen passengers occupied the aft.

A banquet held on Mark Twain's birthday, November 30, closed the centennial celebrations. Clara Frazier, the granddaughter of Laura Hawkins Frazier (a childhood friend of Mark Twain's and one of his inspirations for the character of Becky Thatcher), cut the birthday cake.

SPANNING THE MISSISSIPPI

When word spread in the early 1930s that federal funds were to be appropriated by the new president, Franklin Delano Roosevelt, to finance civic projects across the country, leaders in Hannibal quickly sprang to action. It had long been believed that a bridge across the Mississippi at Hannibal would be a big boon to the local economy. Such a bridge might

The original Mark Twain Memorial Bridge (upper right) led traffic on U.S. 36 straight into the downtown area. *Courtesy Steve Chou.*

be situated so that people traveling by automobile would be led directly into downtown Hannibal, boosting revenue to businesses and stores in the area.

With the support of Hannibal civic leaders and local and state government officials, it was announced that $850,000 in federal funds had been appropriated for the new bridge in June 1933. The following year, buildings at the foot of Cardiff Hill were being demolished (where the bridge would come into Hannibal). The bridge would span 2,636 feet from Missouri to Illinois, with piers sunk 57 feet into solid rock below the surface of the Mississippi to support its weight.

In August 1936, tickets were sold for the bridge's opening to be held on September 4. President Roosevelt would personally appear at the dedication ceremony to cut a ribbon held by the governors of Missouri and Illinois. A contest was held for local girls to see who could sell the most tickets, and the winner would be allowed to present a ticket to the president. Thirty-two girls competed for the honor; fourteen-year-old Louisa McMein was the winner.

Hannibal-LaGrange College was relocated to Hannibal from LaGrange, Missouri, in 1928. Above is the earliest building on the new campus. *Courtesy Steve Chou.*

A parade was held to celebrate the dedication of the Mark Twain Memorial Bridge. President Roosevelt, Missouri senator Harry S Truman, Missouri governor Guy Park and other dignitaries rode in the procession. The dedication drew more than seventy-five thousand people from several states.

HANNIBAL AND THE WAR EFFORT

In July 1940, Missouri governor Lloyd Stark appointed Scott Meyer of Hannibal to the State Industrial Commission, a ten-member group formed to investigate the possibility of bringing defense manufacturing to Missouri. Although President Franklin D. Roosevelt told the nation, "We are preparing to keep the peace," most realized that war was imminent, and the United States was ill prepared. Manufacturing plants would have to be converted for military production, and new industry would also be funded to provide defense. It would help pull Missouri out of the Great Depression to bring jobs and industry to the area.

One of the first industries in Hannibal to convert to wartime production was the International Shoe Company. In 1940, it employed twenty-five hundred workers, whose payroll totaled more than $2 million. In 1941, it began to convert its shoe production to the use of wooden heels (as rubber would be needed for the war effort). Up to fifteen thousand shoes were produced per day. The Bluff City factory also converted to defense manufacturing by producing men's shoes. In 1943, it began rebuilding shoes for the United States Army, employing more than eight hundred workers, who could refurbish as many as six thousand pairs per day.

Durasteel, which had retooled in early 1940 to produce lawn furniture, instead began filling an order for more than 100,000 M47A1 chemical bombs in 1942. Of Durasteel's one hundred employees during the war, thirty-seven of them were women. (After the war, the Durasteel plant converted back to manufacturing metal porch furniture.)

Donald M. Nelson, Hannibal High School class of 1906, was made executive director of the Supply, Priorities and Allocation Board by President Roosevelt on September 2, 1941. He later became the director of the War Production Board, responsible for transitioning manufacturing and industry to production for the war effort. Because of the duties of his office, Nelson was actually superior in rank to Vice President Henry Wallace and Secretary of the Navy Frank Knox; he was also featured on the cover of *Time* magazine on February 2, 1942, with the cover story entitled, "Nelson Takes Over." Throughout the war, Nelson was able to consistently meet production goals of sixty thousand planes, thirty thousand tanks and 86 million tons of steel to provide to the armed forces.

After the bombing of Pearl Harbor on December 7, 1941, Hannibal joined the rest of the nation in support of the war. Civilian defense measures were practiced, including the use of camouflage. To prevent light from being seen during blackout drills, Hannibal housewives hung heavy, dark drapes and blinds in their windows. The Red Cross raised funds, and defense savings bonds were purchased from local banks. Rationing of sugar, coffee, meat, canned goods, butter, tires, typewriters, shoes and nylons was instituted. Victory gardens were planted. Metals for ammunition and rubber for tires on military vehicles were donated to the war effort. On Christmas Day 1942, the local telephone company asked residents to limit long-distance phone usage to enable servicemen to call home.

In March 1942, Samuel Glenn Fuqua, who lived at 401 North Fifth Street in Hannibal, was awarded the Congressional Medal of Honor by President Roosevelt. *Life* magazine reported on Fuqua in its March 30 issue:

> *Samuel Glenn Fuqua—This Navy lieutenant commander was awarded the Congressional Medal of Honor. Knocked down and stunned by explosions in his ship, the* Arizona, *he braved repeated enemy bombing and strafing attacks to get to the quarterdeck. From there he directed fire fighting while wounded were being removed. He remained aboard until satisfied that all who could be had been saved, and then left the* Arizona *with the last boatload.*

In September 1943, a War Bond drive came to Hannibal. A glamorous troop of Hollywood movie stars arrived by train to encourage the purchase of bonds, including Mickey Rooney, Judy Garland, James Cagney, Greer Garson, Betty Hutton, Lucille Ball, Fred Astaire and Harpo Marx. More than $1 million was raised. Other War Bond drives were held in Hannibal throughout the war—a total of more than $8 million in bonds were eventually purchased in Hannibal.

In the fall of 1944, 265 German prisoners of war were brought by train to Hannibal from Clarinda, Iowa, for a six-week project. More than two million shoes had been donated to the war effort from all across the country, and the Germans were brought to Hannibal to aid in sorting the shoes and preparing them for repair. Bluff City Shoe Company had received the U.S. Army's contract to refurbish the shoes, which would then be sent to Europe. The Europeans (particularly those in Greece) would receive the repaired shoes, as their countries had been devastated by the war and all essentials were needed to help them rebuild their lives.

Clemens Field was converted into a temporary encampment for the prisoners, who lived in tents behind a barbed-wire fence inside the compound. By all accounts, the German POWs were well received in Hannibal. There was great mistrust throughout the country of the Japanese because of the bombing of Pearl Harbor, but most Americans did not harbor the same resentment for Germans. Bread and fresh vegetables were regularly brought to the camp by Hannibal residents concerned for the Germans' well-being. There was even talk that the POWs might be allowed to attend a football game at Hannibal High School, but the U.S. Army vetoed the idea. One

Hannibal resident recalled groups of locals gathering at the edge of the bluff at the end of South Fifth Street to listen to the prisoners singing as they sat around their evening campfires.

The language barrier caused a bit of a stir with the German POWs. As reported by the Hagoods in *The Story of Hannibal*:

> *On one occasion they* [the POWs] *asked for raw sausage, a traditional delicacy in their homes. The request was denied with a warning that raw sausage might cause trichinosis. Due to the language difference, they misunderstood, and feared they were all being poisoned or fed wormy meat. This misunderstanding was finally cleared up by a butcher who spoke German.*

On April 12, 1945, President Roosevelt died, and Missouri's own Harry S Truman was sworn into office as the thirty-third president of the United States. Hannibal mayor W.J. Schneider proclaimed April 14 as a day of mourning for Roosevelt. Citizens gathered in Central Park for services, including five minutes of meditative silence and the ringing of church bells.

In August 1945, the war came to an end with the surrender of Japan. On "V-J Day," the *Courier-Post* reported on the jubilant celebration in Hannibal:

> *When the announcement came over the radio and Associated Press wire at 6 p.m., there was little noise to be heard on the streets. Within minutes the scene changed. Folks who had waited so long for the news evidently stuffed the remaining bits of their evening meal into their mouths and got out their automobiles, caring little if they had but one gasoline stamp left, and drove to the business section to join in the celebration.*

OUT WITH THE OLD, IN WITH THE NEW

After the war in the late 1940s and early '50s, Hannibalians were moving into the Atomic Age. The trend across the United States during this time was to abandon the old and look toward a shiny, bright new future. Technological and mechanical advancements were changing the way Americans lived their daily lives, altering the very nature of how we worked and played as a nation.

One example was the advent of television. Fred W. Simmons, who lived at 1007 Paris Avenue, owned the first television in Hannibal. His small unit was able to pick up signals from St. Louis stations, and he premiered his television set to friends on October 11, 1947.

New subdivisions were being built west of Highway 61, and every family had an automobile. Rather than walking to shop, people began to drive their cars. Parking, especially downtown, became a challenge. As some of the old downtown buildings showed signs of decline, they were razed in favor of parking lots. The old Planters Hotel at 319 North Main Street, built in 1836, was dismantled in 1954, along with adjoining buildings, to make room for parking. One of the buildings razed had once been the offices of the *Missouri Courier*, where Samuel Clemens had learned the printing trade in the late 1840s and early '50s.

Other buildings were also brought down. The Farmers Elevator and Exchange building on South Third Street was demolished during the 1950s, along with 115 South Main, the Helm building at Third and Hill Streets and Dr. Bank's home on Fifth Street, now the parking lot for the Hannibal Free Public Library. In 1953, the landmark Union Depot was razed and replaced with a new, smaller depot for Burlington (later known as BNSF).

Public schools in Hannibal also changed drastically in the late 1950s. School buses were first implemented in 1957, transporting students to Hannibal High School, Central School, Eugene Field Elementary, Mark Twain Elementary and Douglass School. Four buses were purchased by the school district in 1957, with another in 1958 and two more in 1959. Desegregation was also instituted during this time. The last graduation ceremony at Douglass School was in the spring of 1955. That fall, students were matriculated into Hannibal High School. Douglass continued to hold classes for the elementary and junior high school students until 1959, when the students were transferred to other Hannibal public schools. The conversion from segregated to integrated schools occurred with only minor difficulty and finally brought equality in education to young Hannibalians.

TOM SAWYER DAYS

In 1955, the Hannibal Jaycees began to develop the idea for a large-scale celebration to be held annually in Hannibal. The first Tom Sawyer Day was held on August 18, 1956. The event included a picnic and riverfront show. A parade down Broadway was held, with marching bands, horsemen from the Saddleview Club and seven floats featuring characters from Mark Twain's writings. The highlight of the day featured boys lining up in front of the white picket fence near Mark Twain's boyhood home to compete in the fence-painting contest. Dennis Reed of Jefferson City won first prize.

At the first Tom Sawyer Day in 1956, the chairman of the Tourist Development Committee, George Pace, announced the appointment of Chris Winkler and Perva Lou Smith as the city's official Tom and Becky. They would serve as representatives of the characters, in costume, at civic functions throughout the year.

The next year, at the second Tom Sawyer Day celebration, a competition was held for the new Tom and Becky that included a test for knowledge of Hannibal's history. The winners, Jimmie Gentry and Jean Richmond, were announced. Actor Hal Holbrook came to Hannibal and joined in the festivities. Holbrook had begun to perform his one-man show, *Mark Twain Tonight,* in 1954. Appearing as Mark Twain, Holbrook remained in

Fence-painting contests are part of the National Tom Sawyer Days festival, first held in 1956. *Courtesy Steve Chou.*

character throughout the Tom Sawyer Day celebration. The event gained national attention.

In 1958, the title "National Tom Sawyer Days" was given congressional recognition, facilitated by Missouri's U.S. senators Stuart Symington and Edward Long. One year later, the Hannibal Chamber of Commerce joined the Hannibal Jaycees by combining Hannibal's Fourth of July celebration, sponsored by the chamber, with the National Tom Sawyer Days. Since that time, the National Tom Sawyer Days celebration has always been held over the July 4 weekend, regularly attracting tens of thousands of people from all over the world to participate in events such as mud volleyball, an antique car show, a large arts and crafts fair in Central Park, frog-jumping contests and, of course, fence-painting contests. The annual Tom and Becky contest draws dozens of hopeful seventh grade boys and girls from Hannibal to compete for the title; to be named the "official" Tom and Becky is a highly coveted honor (alternate pairs of Tom and Beckys are named and serve throughout the year as well). A massive fireworks display launched from Lover's Leap is the highlight of the festivities.

Hannibal in the 1960s

In June 1960, an enormous windstorm with seventy-mile-per-hour gusts blew apart the lighthouse on Cardiff Hill. When the structure was originally built in 1935, designers had only planned for it to be in place for twenty-five years. By the time of the storm, the lighthouse had become part of Hannibal's landscape, and many wished to see it restored. Funds were raised by public subscription in a drive spearheaded by E.L. Sparks Jr., and the newly constructed lighthouse was dedicated on May 24, 1963. At the ceremony, Hannibal Girl and Boy Scouts formed a "Spiral of Light," lighting a series of candles that extended from the base of the steps up to the top (244 stairs). The beacon light atop the lighthouse was donated by the United States Coast Guard and was ceremoniously lit by President John F. Kennedy at the White House in the same manner as the original dedication in 1935 by Roosevelt.

In March 1962, the International Shoe Company plant on Seventh Street closed its doors after the company decided to consolidate its manufacturing in another location. Further pullout came in 1964, when it halted the manufacturing of shoes in the Bluff City plant. The Rubber Plant, which made heels and soles for International Shoe, closed its doors in 1967. The closing of these facilities was the end of an era that spanned more than sixty years of significant shoe manufacturing in Hannibal.

A new development brought substantial change to Hannibal in 1965. That year, Hannibal's first shopping district away from the downtown area, the Huck Finn Center, opened. The National Chain Store Leases, Inc., of St. Louis built the strip mall on a thirty-acre site on McMasters Avenue (Highway 61). Some stores that leased space in the Huck Finn Center were new to Hannibal, but others were businesses that previously had been located downtown. The convenience of shopping in a concentrated area with modern buildings and spacious parking areas appealed to most Hannibalians. The shift in the shopping habits of the residents of Hannibal was significant, and shops on Broadway and Main Street saw a serious decline in traffic when the Huck Finn Center was opened for business.

Downtown suffered a second setback during the flood of 1965. On May 1, the river levels had risen to 24.59 feet and might have gone even higher if not for a levee failure upriver near Quincy. At the intersection of Main and Center Streets, water was reported to be 3.00 feet deep inside the buildings. The muddy floodwaters made the lure of moving downtown businesses from Broadway and Main Street closer to the traffic of Highway 61 even more attractive.

Hannibalians literally watch the river flow down Main Street during the 1965 flood. A levee protecting businesses along Main Street was completed in late 1992. *Courtesy Steve Chou.*

Tragedy in the Caves

On May 10, 1967, three boys set out to go cave exploring. The boys—thirteen-year-old Joey Hoag; his ten-year-old little brother, Bill; and their friend Craig Dowell, age fourteen—had spent many days playing in the caves, usually in a section called Murphy's Cave in South Hannibal. As they made their way with shovels and flashlights, they stopped for a moment to say hello to some of the Hannibal firemen on duty at the fire station. And then they disappeared.

When the parents reported the boys missing later that evening, a massive search and rescue began that would eventually include thousands of volunteers. Members of the Speleological Society of America, the National Capitol Underground Rescue Squad of Washington, D.C., and the Hondo Underground Rescue Team joined in the search. Missouri National Guard and Civil Defense Unit servicemen were deployed. Policemen, firefighters and other emergency personnel from several states were also sent to Hannibal to aid in the search. Hundreds of volunteers supplied food and water to rescue workers so that the search could be conducted around the clock.

At the time of the boys' disappearance, the highway department was building a road on the western slopes of Lover's Leap as part of a scenic route of Highway 79. Construction crews had unearthed several holes that revealed a cave system inside the bluff of Lover's Leap, and it was feared that the boys might have attempted a very dangerous exploration of these openings. Murphy's Cave was also included in the search. Eventually, volunteers fanned out and investigated a seven-mile radius around Hannibal's city limits; 272 mines, quarries, holes and other possible cave entrances were explored. All vacant houses and buildings in Hannibal were searched, as was the entire sewer system. On the Mississippi, all islands between the southern shores of Hannibal and Lock & Dam #22 were searched. Approximately 250 national guardsmen spread out and searched the empty structures, barns, sheds, railroad cars and freight trains in the area. The boys' disappearance was reported in news broadcasts across the country.

The official search lasted eighteen days at a cost of more than $1 million, but no sign of the missing boys was ever found. After the search and rescue was called off, all entrances to the cave under Lover's Leap were sealed.

On the twenty-fifth anniversary of the disappearance, in May 1992, a granite memorial was laid at the top of Lover's Leap to commemorate the lives of the three young boys.

HANNIBAL SESQUICENTENNIAL

A group of Hannibal citizens approached Mayor Harry Musgrove during the summer of 1968 with a plan. The 150th anniversary of the founding of Hannibal was coming up, and it was believed that a celebration should take place. The group wanted to solicit the mayor's support and believed that no outside planners were required; Hannibal had enough of its own talent to produce the event. Mayor Musgrove gave his consent, and planning of the yearlong event quickly commenced. Hannibal Festivals, Inc., was formed, with Jerry Sampson as chairman.

A wide variety of events were scheduled. An official emblem for the sesquicentennial was designed that would be featured on coins, souvenirs and a pictorial booklet of Hannibal's history. Two Hannibal youths, Joe Welch and Jim Bridges, planned to build a raft and float down the Mississippi to distribute flyers about the event to river towns all the way down to Portage de Sioux. The celebration was underway.

The festival opened on February 7, 1969. It was decided that a special distinction should be given to the first baby born after the opening ceremony. The Sesquicentennial Baby was Tanya Sue King, born at 8:52 a.m. on February 8.

The main events of the celebration took place during National Tom Sawyer Days in July. Men were encouraged to grow beards to celebrate the "pioneer spirit." A plan was devised to attempt to break the world's record for flagpole sitting. The Wagon Wheel Saddle Club and Hannibal Jaycees performed a reenactment of the Pony Express.

An essay contest was held to determine the Sesquicentennial Prince and Princess, and contestants were asked to write how they could best contribute to the community of Hannibal. Steven Stout and Janie Greening were crowned after submitting the winning entries. The Crèpe Paper Ball, held at Rockcliffe Mansion, was a major success. The pageant *Hannibaltown* was performed at the high school stadium. And, of course, there was fence painting and a parade down Broadway.

The closing event of the sesquicentennial was the burial of a time capsule in Central Park. Bob Bush, Gary Freeman and the newly elected mayor Fred Herrin did the honors. The time capsule is scheduled to be reopened on Hannibal's 200th birthday in 2019.

In 1972, the Mark Twain Cave was named a Registered National Natural Landmark by the National Park Service, noting that it was one of the most exceptional examples of "maze"-type caves in the country.

The cave was made famous by Mark Twain, first in *The Adventures of Tom Sawyer*, but also mentioned in four other books by Twain. The first tour guide of the cave was John East, who charged ten cents per person. Evan T. Cameron served as guide from 1886 through 1944, charging twenty-five cents for adults and ten cents for children. These early tours distinguish the Mark Twain Cave as being the oldest show cave in Missouri.

Today, the Mark Twain Cave is part of a complex that includes Cameron Cave, campground facilities and retail shops. The complex is one of the top attractions in Hannibal, visited by tens of thousands of guests each year.

The Flood of 1973

The Mississippi River reached a new record height of 28.59 feet on April 25, 1973, the greatest flood to date. The trouble began with the melting of heavy winter snows followed by early spring rains that began to elevate the river levels in mid-March. An initial crest of 23.45 feet pushed water into the downtown area on March 28, but the water receded, and the river returned to its normal depths within a few days. Some thought the worst was over. Sadly, heavy rain began on April 20 and would drop nearly seven inches of rain over the next several days. The river again began to rise, and by Easter Sunday, April 22, it was apparent that the river was threatening one of the worst floods in recorded history.

Water began to flow into downtown. It crept up Broadway to the alley between Main and Third Street, and all the buildings on Main Street were flooded. In many storefronts, the water level reached as high as six feet deep. After the crest on April 25, property owners began to assess the damage using rowboats down Main Street; motorboats could not be used because the wake that was created might further damage the structures.

After each devastating flood, it would always take months of cleanup before things could return to normal. Mud and debris had to be hauled away, buildings reinforced and repainted and stores restocked. But during

The 1973 flood reached a crest of 28.59 feet, filling the buildings along Main Street with up to 6.00 feet of water. *Courtesy Steve Chou.*

the flood of 1973, the worst outcome was the loss of the Hannibal Board of Public Works' Electric Generating Plant on Front Street. The flood damaged the plant beyond repair, and the city lost its ability to generate its own electricity.

People were relieved when the devastation of the flood of 1973 was finally behind them. Most believed there would never be another flood to match the record-breaking flood of '73; unfortunately, it would only be twenty years before the river would reach an even greater depth in Hannibal.

Hannibal celebrated with the rest of the nation in 1976 to commemorate the 200th anniversary of the signing of the Declaration of Independence. One significant event that was held for the first time that year would become a lasting annual affair: the Historic Life Festival (currently called the Folklife Festival), sponsored each October by the Hannibal Arts Council.

The council had been formed just one year earlier in 1975. As a civic project and fundraising opportunity, the Historic Life (Folklife) Festival's main features are the artisans who travel to Hannibal from far and wide to produce and sell heritage arts and crafts. Civic groups from Hannibal and neighboring communities offer concessions that befit the theme of the event, including kettle corn, chicken and dumplings, roast turkey legs and old-fashioned lemonade. Folk music is played by street vendors wandering the festival; gunfight reenactments and theatrical presentations add to the old-timey atmosphere. The Folklife Festival is now a widely popular event, with tens of thousands of visitors attending the two-day celebration that takes place each fall on historic Main Street. In 2010, the executive director of the Hannibal Arts Council, Michael Gaines, accepted the Missouri Tourism Board's Spotlight Award, given for noteworthy contributions in "spotlighting" Missouri tourism. The award was to celebrate the success of the Hannibal Arts Council's annual Folklife Festival.

Hannibal has been fortunate to have received many United States presidents through the years, including Abraham Lincoln, William Henry Harrison, Ulysses S. Grant, Teddy Roosevelt, Franklin Delano Roosevelt and Harry S Truman. On August 23, 1979, then-president Jimmy Carter, first lady Rosalynn and their daughter, Amy, arrived on the shores of Hannibal aboard the riverboat *Delta Queen* as a stop on their trek down the Mississippi River. The Carter family spent the better part of the day exploring Hannibal. Henry Sweets III, curator of the Mark Twain Boyhood Home and Museum, served as tour guide. William Garnett, president of the Mark Twain Home Board, presented Amy with a copy of *The Adventures of Tom Sawyer*. Hurley and Roberta Hagood also presented their book, *The Story of Hannibal*, to President and Mrs. Carter. A motorcade ushered the first family to Mark Twain Cave, and after a tour, the Carters again boarded the *Delta Queen* to resume their voyage downriver.

Twain Sesquicentennial

Hannibal is known throughout the world as the hometown of Mark Twain and the setting for *The Adventures of Tom Sawyer* and *Adventures of Huckleberry Finn*. The year 1985 would mark the 150th anniversary of Mark Twain's birth, and Hannibal could not pass up the opportunity for a large-scale event to celebrate the life and legacy of its native son.

Hannibal mayor John Lyng and the city council appointed a Sesquicentennial Committee of thirteen members to plan the celebration, with Larry Weil as chairman. A grand plan was envisioned that would stretch from May 4 until the close of the event on Mark Twain's birthday, November 30. In an effort to attract national attention, major events were scattered across the schedule, including nationally known musical groups, television personalities and other entertainers who would be commissioned to perform. To pay for the festivities, sponsorship from major corporations would be sought.

Unfortunately, not all of the Sesquicentennial Committee's plans came to fruition. Corporate sponsors did not prove to be as generous as hoped, and conflicts arose between some of the event's coordinators. Some plans were scaled back, and a few of the major events were cancelled. Despite the setbacks, the celebration encompassed the entire summer and fall of 1985 and attracted many first-time visitors to Hannibal.

The star of the show was most definitely Mark Twain. Two costumed characters greeted visitors on Main Street: Hannibal the Frog (from *Twain's Celebrated Jumping Frog of Calaveras County*, also the inspiration for the event's slogan, "Hannibal's Jumping!") and Aunt Polly (from *The Adventures of Tom Sawyer*).

The Mark Twain Writers Conference was held at Hannibal-LaGrange College the week of June 17, featuring many prestigious lecturers, including Pulitzer Prize winners Justin Kaplan, author of *Mr. Clemens and Mark Twain*, and Hannibal's own Ron Powers.

The Mark Twain Museum received two special donations during the sesquicentennial: *Mark Twain in His Later Years* (writing while reclining in bed) by St. Louis sculptor Don Weigand and another Twain likeness by local artist Father Louis McCorkle. In October, the Visitors' Center was honored to display a special Mark Twain exhibition supplied by the Smithsonian Institution.

Three official parades were held down Broadway on May 4 (at the opening of the festivities), the Fourth of July and Labor Day. Other smaller groups paraded down Main Street throughout the summer. Spectacular fireworks displays appeared in the skies over Hannibal after many of the larger events.

The Riverfront Amphitheater, a new venue located in Nipper Park along the riverfront, had been constructed specifically for the sesquicentennial. Performances by the St. Louis Symphony, Doc Severinsen, Air Supply, trumpeter Al Hirt, the Beach Boys, the Oak Ridge Boys, the Osmonds, Survivor, the United States Army Band and many others drew large crowds all summer.

Many other events were held: paddleboat races, performances by Mark Twain reenactor Bill McLinn, quilting contests, antique and classic car shows, street dances, a petting zoo, a reunion of railroad enthusiasts, a Pork-o-rama food fest and a wine festival. National Tom Sawyer Days were held in conjunction with the sesquicentennial, with Eric Durr and Elizabeth Brown named that year's Tom and Becky. The Historic Life Festival was sponsored in October by the Hannibal Arts Council and featured more than three hundred vendors. Even the Goodyear Blimp made an appearance over the skies of Hannibal.

On September 12, three of the premier steamboats on the Mississippi—the legendary *Delta Queen*, the *Mississippi Queen* and the *New Orleans*—docked together on Hannibal's shore. Passengers were treated to a catfish and cornbread meal on the riverfront.

President Ronald Reagan declared November 30, 1985, National Mark Twain Day, bringing the sesquicentennial to a close. The 150th anniversary of the birth of Mark Twain was celebrated in many cities across America and throughout the world, but certainly the epicenter of the celebration was located in Hannibal, Missouri.

THE FLOOD OF 1993

Flooding in Hannibal has always been a major concern. In 1964, and again in 1975, after most Hannibalians thought the greatest flood in their lifetimes had occurred in 1973, proposals were brought forth to build a levee to protect downtown Hannibal. But it wasn't until December 1986 that a plan for a levee system was formally endorsed by the Hannibal City Council.

The estimated cost of the project was $5.8 million. Bleigh Construction Company of Hannibal submitted the winning bid for the project and commenced construction on April 10, 1990. The plan called for a levee wall stretching 3,650 feet long and 12 feet high, replacing what used to be Front Street. The wall would allow traffic to enter the riverfront area with a system of removable steel bulkheads, or floodgates, each measuring 40 feet long by 13 feet high and weighing eleven tons. One removable gate was at the foot of Hill Street, another at the foot of Center Street, a third at the Broadway approach to the riverfront and the fourth at the south end of Main Street to protect downtown from the flooding of Bear Creek. The levee wall project was complete in the fall of 1992.

In the months between January and March 1993, there was no indication that the largest flood ever recorded on the Mississippi was on its way down the river. Rainfall in those months was only slightly above normal. In late March, the rain picked up, and the Mississippi rose above flood stage on March 18, cresting at 19.59 feet. The rise in river levels lasted only five days before again falling below flood stage. However, in April, 5.07 inches of rain fell. The Army Corps of Engineers recommended that the gates be put into place if the river rose above 18.60 feet, and on April 16, the floodgates were installed for the very first time. On April 23, the river had risen to just over 24.00 feet; it fell slightly, only to rise to 24.15 feet on April 27. The river continued the pattern of rising and falling as it absorbed more than 10.00 inches of rain in May. Finally, on May 21, river levels had finally dropped far enough for the floodgates to be removed.

The excess water from the river flowed into Bear Creek, flooding homes that were not protected by the floodgates along South Main Street and east of Sycamore, as well as on Ely Street along the Bear Creek flood plain. Marion County was declared a disaster area. It was a relief, however, that the first test of the levee confirmed that historic Main Street was now being protected from flooding.

Most believed that the worst of the flooding was over. Unfortunately, the heavy northern snows that fell in the winter of 1992–93 began to finally be carried south by the Mississippi River in late May. The worst was yet to come.

On June 24, the floodgates were again installed, and by July 1, the citizens of Hannibal began to brace for another record-setting flood. The river was expected to crest at 29.00 feet on July 3, topping the 1973 record flood stage of 28.59 feet. National Tom Sawyer Days events were relocated away from the riverfront that weekend, and the Mark Twain Bridge that crossed the river into Illinois was closed due to the flooding of the bridge's entrance ramps. The National Guard was called up on July 5 to help with disaster relief.

The river broke its previous record depth on July 8, reaching 28.7 feet. However, the crest was not predicted to occur until three days later, with estimates as high as 32.0 feet, roughly double the Mississippi's average normal depth in Hannibal. Citizens were asked to volunteer to assist with filling sand bags to raise the height of the levee and floodgates an additional 2.0 feet. The new levee was built to withstand a 32.0-foot flood, a level that no one thought would ever be reached.

The all-time high-water mark of the Mississippi River in Hannibal occurred at 9:00 p.m. on July 25, 1993, when flood levels reached the astonishing depth of 31.8 feet, breaking the twenty-year-old record by more than 3.0 feet. Many levees along the Mississippi River in Iowa, Illinois and Missouri failed, but Hannibal's new levee held firm. By August 12, the river had fallen to just over 20.0 feet, and the floodgates were finally removed on September 21 after the river returned to a more normal depth of only 15.7 feet.

Even with the levee's success, the floodwaters had devastated Hannibal residents and businesses along Bear Creek. Three hundred acres in Hannibal were flooded, many under ten feet of water for more than a month and most from the flooding of Bear Creek to the south. Federal and state agencies sent personnel to assist with the cleanup, but in some areas the devastation was so extreme that the property owners did not return even after the water began to recede.

It is remarkable to think that the levee was completed just a few months before the Mississippi River began to rise in what would become the greatest flood in its recorded history. It is widely believed that if the levee had not been in place, the river would have so overwhelmed Hannibal's Main Street that the buildings we cherish, including Mark Twain's Boyhood Home, would no longer stand. The saturation of the foundations and the length of time that the water would have been standing in those areas would have weakened the structures to the point that they would no longer be inhabitable. But because of the levee and the steel floodgates, Main Street remained dry. Hannibal's historic district had been spared.

On September 16, 2000, the new Mark Twain Memorial Bridge was dedicated. The four-lane bridge, with a price tag of $55 million, joined U.S. Highway 36 with Interstate 72 and spanned the Mississippi to Illinois, thus replacing the original Mark Twain Bridge that was dedicated by Franklin D. Roosevelt in 1936. A crowd of more than ten thousand walked the bridge, later gathering at Nipper Park, where a large television screen had been erected to broadcast the ceremonies. Tom Boland, Hannibal businessman and former leader of the Missouri Highway Commission, performed the master of ceremonies duty and introduced Governor Mel Carnahan, Senators Kit Bond and John Ashcroft, Representative Harold Volkmer, Hannibal mayor Robert Moloney and many other dignitaries. Bands played, and a massive American flag was raised. Robert Clayton, portraying Mark Twain, was the first to cross the bridge driving a Model T Ford.

The 1936 bridge began to be dismantled on January 8, 2001. The bridge was imploded, section by section, and the pieces retrieved from the Mississippi for salvage.

❧

Today, Hannibal is considered a small, rural, northeastern Missouri town, with a population that hovers just over seventeen thousand. Old blends with new, and families whose Hannibal roots go back for generations live alongside "transplants" who have chosen to make Hannibal their new home. The community is diverse, represented by a broad range of ethnicities and socioeconomic backgrounds.

As Twain's popularity throughout the world continues, so, too, does the interest in Hannibal, visited by tens of thousands of Twain enthusiasts each year. There is a responsibility that all Hannibalians share in maintaining the heritage of Twain's hometown so as to preserve its legacy for future generations. Through the efforts of historians and preservationists over the last one hundred years, much of Hannibal has, in fact, been preserved. The preservation of Hannibal continues today. According to Arthur Frommer in *Preservation Forum* (1988):

> *Every study of travel motivations has shown that an interest in the achievements of the past is among the three major reasons why people travel...those that have substantially preserved their past continue to enjoy tourism...Tourism does not go to a city that has lost its soul.*

HISTORIC PRESERVATION

During the 1950s and '60s, many Hannibal buildings were lost to the wrecking ball. Old buildings were torn down for new, modern structures or, even worse, parking lots. In the late 1960s, when the drug culture surfaced and Vietnam made Americans question the status quo, people began to look back to a simpler, gentler time. Shows on public television stations popped up, teaching us how to lovingly restore our old houses. The wave of historic preservation began to emerge and was highlighted during the American bicentennial in 1976, when history—American history—was brought back into the popular mainstream.

Hannibal, even today, continues to lose some of its most architecturally interesting structures. Hannibal was fortunate, however, that many of its residents, from early on, realized the importance of our American heritage and spent considerable time and money to preserve sites that make Hannibal unique. Volumes could be written on preservation efforts in Hannibal. For a town of only 17,500 citizens, remarkably, Hannibal has four distinct historic districts: the Central Business Historic District, featuring the buildings of Main Street; the Mark Twain Boyhood Home Complex; the Maple Avenue Historic District, featuring many fine examples of nineteenth- and early twentieth-century architecture, including Rockcliffe and Cliffside Mansions; and the Central Park Historic District, which includes the mansions of Millionaires' Row (Fifth Street) and other mid- to late nineteenth-century Victorian homes and structures. Today, the National Register of Historic

Places recognizes nearly one hundred buildings as part of these four historic districts, all because of a phenomenal effort previously put forth by preservationists and historians to protect and preserve this quintessential Mississippi River town.

MARK TWAIN BOYHOOD HOME AND MUSEUM COMPLEX

The assemblage of historic structures and sites that exemplify Hannibal as it was during Samuel Clemens's boyhood were brought together piece by piece over the last one hundred years and now compose the Mark Twain Boyhood Home and Museum Complex. The complex includes the Mark Twain Boyhood Home and Gardens, Becky Thatcher's House, John Marshall Clemens's justice of the peace office, Pilaster House/Grant's Drugstore, the Interpretive Center, the Tom and Huck Statue, Huckleberry Finn's House and the Mark Twain Museum Gallery.

One year after Mark Twain's death, in 1911, Hannibalian George A. Mahan purchased the small, two-story frame building near the corner of Hill and Main Streets. The structure had been poorly maintained, and if it had not been rescued, it would have become a butcher shop.

Mahan was one of the first to sense the importance that Mark Twain's legacy was to have on the small, rural community of Hannibal. As so nicely stated by the Hagoods in their book *Hannibal, Too*, "The foresight of the Mahans in preserving the Mark Twain Boyhood Home provided the city with a facility which became a worldwide shrine to the memory of Mark Twain." The Mark Twain Boyhood Home, originally built in 1843, was presented by the Mahan family to the City of Hannibal and dedicated in a large ceremony on May 15, 1912.

With a vision for a monument to celebrate Hannibal's most famous (fictional) sons, Mahan would enlist the talents of Frederick Hibbard. Hibbard, no stranger to Hannibal, had previously completed a remarkable statue of Mark Twain that was installed in Riverview Park. Mahan asked Hibbard to sculpt a statue of Huck and Tom, the first public statue in America devoted to fictional characters, to be placed at the foot of Cardiff Hill at the northern end of Main Street. The Mahan family donated this statue to the City of Hannibal in a dedication ceremony on May 27, 1926.

Gathering in front of the Mark Twain Boyhood Home on April 25, 1935, for the Centennial Celebration are (left to right) George A. Mahan, Morris Anderson, Clara Clemens Gabrilowitsch (Twain's daughter), Ralph Roberson (Huck Finn), Pary Nash (Becky Thatcher), sculptor Walter Russell, Buddy Flick (Tom Sawyer) and Nina Gabrilowitsch (Twain's granddaughter). *Courtesy Steve Chou.*

George A. Mahan would serve as president of the Missouri State Historical Society for a number of years. His interest in history and preservation would prove invaluable to Hannibal. After purchasing Mark Twain's boyhood home, Mahan would go on to purchase and restore the circa 1840 Pilaster House at the corner of Hill and Main Streets. This historically significant building is where the Clemens family lived for a time in an upstairs apartment and is also where John Marshall Clemens died in 1847. Sarah Marshall Mahan, George's daughter-in-law, donated the property to the City of Hannibal in 1956, and it was restored and opened to the public in 1959. Today, it features a historically accurate representation of mid-nineteenth-century Grant's Drugstore, and tourists can walk through the first floor as part of the Boyhood Home Complex.

In 1935, the WPA also contributed to the preservation and beautification of the Boyhood Home Complex. A stone structure was built next to the

Boyhood Home that would be home to the Mark Twain Museum, dedicated on November 30, 1937 (Mark Twain's birthday). When the "new" Mark Twain Museum opened in 1997, the stone building was repurposed and now serves as a museum gift shop.

Another WPA project was the construction of the tall stone wall directly behind the Boyhood Home. In the 1930s, the Cruikshank Lumber Company was situated just north of the small frame house. Fear of fire damaging the historic property prompted construction of the wall as a fire barrier between the lumberyard and the Boyhood Home.

George A. Mahan's son, Dulany, passed away in 1940. As a memorial to her husband, Sarah Marshall Mahan facilitated the installation of the gardens next to the Boyhood Home and donated the park to the City of Hannibal in 1941. "This was given to aid in perpetuating the name and fame of that world-beloved author [Mark Twain]," Mrs. Mahan said at the dedication ceremony, "and shall be a memorial to my late husband Dulany D. Mahan."

John Marshall Clemens's justice of the peace office was originally located in the 100 block of Bird Street. In the early 1940s, Warner Bros. was in preproduction for their feature film *The Adventures of Mark Twain* (released in 1944) and spent considerable time in Hannibal doing research. As a "thank you" for the hospitality they received while in Hannibal, Warner Bros. purchased the Clemens Office and donated it to the city on November 30, 1943. In 1956, it was moved to its present location on Hill Street behind Grant's Drugstore, where it was restored and rededicated on Law Day, May 1, 1959, by the Missouri Bar Association. Lieutenant Governor Edward Long gave an address on the life of Judge Clemens at the dedication ceremony.

Also in the 1950s, John Winkler was the man responsible for the restoration of the Becky Thatcher House. The two-story frame structure at 211 Hill Street, built in the 1840s right across from Twain's boyhood home, was originally the home of the Elijah Hawkins family; daughter Laura was a childhood friend of Mark Twain and an inspiration for the character of Becky Thatcher in *The Adventures of Tom Sawyer*. Winkler served for many years as president of the Mark Twain Board and was presented with an engraved silver cup in 1958 by the National Trust for Historic Preservation for his leadership and preservation efforts of the historic buildings and artifacts in the Mark Twain Historic District.

In 1966, the Hannibal City Council voted to allow the 200 block of Hill Street to be closed to traffic and made into a pedestrian-only plaza. In 1972, the area was paved with brick supplied by the Mark Twain Board. The plaza would bring cohesion to the Mark Twain Boyhood Home and Museum Complex.

A former pizza parlor at the corner of Main and North Streets was converted in 1983 to the Mark Twain Museum Annex. The space was redesigned in 2004–5 and now serves as the Interpretive Center, the starting point for the tour of the Boyhood Home Complex. This section of the museum features exhibits on Sam Clemens's time in Hannibal and the effect that Hannibal would have on his writings.

The Sonnenberg Building at the corner of Center and Main Streets is now home to the Mark Twain Museum Gallery. The project began in 1996 and has grown over the years to encompass the entire two-story structure. The first floor features interactive exhibits covering five of Mark Twain's most popular books. The second-floor gallery displays artifacts from Mark Twain's life and features fifteen original Norman Rockwell paintings that were done in the 1930s as illustrations for special editions of *The Adventures of Tom Sawyer* and *Adventures of Huckleberry Finn*.

In the ninety-nine years since the Boyhood Home's dedication, millions of Mark Twain devotees from across the globe have made the pilgrimage to Hannibal to walk in the footsteps of Tom Sawyer and Huck Finn. It was many years before attendance records were kept, but it is known that in the fifty years between 1935 and 1985, more than 6.5 million visitors toured the Mark Twain Boyhood Home and Museum Complex. Tens of thousands of visitors each year still roam the plaza on Hill Street, taking their pictures by the whitewashed fence and retracing the steps of one of America's most enduring figures.

HISTORIC DOWNTOWN HANNIBAL

Over the years, many different groups have been formed to ensure the preservation of the historic buildings in downtown Hannibal. For example, one such group, Historic Hannibal, Inc., was formed in 1974 with Charles Anton III as its president. This group spearheaded the effort to restore areas of North Main Street after the flood of 1973. This is just one example of the many group efforts over the years to save some of Hannibal's most remarkable sites. Other preservation projects have included saving the Old Jail at the corner of Church and Fourth Streets (Byzantine-style architecture, built in 1878) and the restoration of Clemens Field (WPA project from 1935), the Star Theater at 215 South Main Street (built in 1906) and the Mark Twain Hotel at 200 South Main Street (1905). There are dozens of people who should be recognized for their preservation efforts and thousands of square feet of historic downtown buildings that have been saved. To each, we offer our sincere gratitude. Your efforts will preserve historic Hannibal for generations to come.

THE MANSIONS OF HANNIBAL

One of the conundrums faced by today's Hannibal preservationists is how to raise the funds to properly care for the massive homes built in Hannibal during the Gilded Age. When the lumber barons ruled and money flowed freely through Hannibal after the Civil War, wealthy Hannibalians spared no expense when constructing their lavish homes. Most homes built in the Central Park and Maple Avenue Historic Districts were two- and three-story structures with servants' quarters. Many of Hannibal's historic district homes fall into the range of twenty-five hundred to four thousand square feet, but more than two dozen mansions and mini mansions were also constructed that are greater than five thousand square feet.

In today's economy, it is difficult to find the means to manage the upkeep of these amazing structures. Many fell into disrepair throughout the twentieth century, and to begin a large-scale renovation of these structures today can be cost-prohibitive. It is difficult to justify the cost of renovating a thirty-five-hundred-square-foot Italianate in a small, rural town that does not see much of an increase in property values from year to year. Another issue is the strain that would be put on the limited number of painters, carpenters and masons who reside in northeast Missouri; the sheer volume of projects required to restore so many nineteenth-century homes makes wide-scale preservation of the historic districts even more difficult.

Although there are structures in Hannibal that need attention, many fine examples of Queen Anne, Italianate, Second Empire, Georgian and other Victorian architectural styles have been and continue to be preserved. Each day, one can drive through one of Hannibal's four historic districts and find evidence of restoration activity.

One project that seemed to start this trend took shape in 1968. Rockcliffe Mansion (1000 Bird Street), which was originally built in 1900 for lumber baron John J. Cruikshank Jr., had been unoccupied for forty-three years and had fallen into such disrepair that the City of Hannibal, thinking it a safety hazard, wanted to bulldoze the structure. Three prominent Hannibal families—Mr. and Mrs. Delbert Hartley, Mr. and Mrs. Joseph C. Raible and Dr. and Mrs. Merrill Roller—purchased the 13,500-square-foot Georgian mansion and, with an army of volunteers, restored the home with the intent to open it to the public for tours. The mansion became a perfectly preserved example of turn-of-the-century architecture (no major renovations had ever been done) and included many artifacts from the original family.

In 1974, another restoration effort began to save the Garth Woodside Mansion (11069 New London Gravel Road). The twenty-room mansion was originally built in 1872 for John H. Garth as a summer home, located approximately three miles from downtown Hannibal. (Garth's winter residence was a six-thousand-square-foot Italianate located on Millionaires' Row at 213 South Fifth Street). Six families purchased the Woodside Mansion property and were responsible for the restoration: Mr. and Mrs. Roy Goodhart, Mr. and Mrs.

The W.B. Pettibone mansion just after its completion in 1912. Today, the property is referred to as Cliffside Mansion. *Courtesy Steve Chou.*

Robert Graham, Mr. and Mrs. James Woollen, Mr. and Mrs. James Boling, Mr. and Mrs. George Johann and Mr. and Mrs. William Beckley. After restoration was complete in 1975, the group opened the mansion to the public for tours.

Other mansions in Hannibal have also been restored. Some now offer bed-and-breakfast accommodations, such as the David Dubach House at 221 North Fifth Street (Italianate/Second Empire, circa 1871), the W.B. Pettibone House at 313 North Fifth Street (Queen Anne, circa 1889), the John L. RoBards Mansion at 215 North Sixth Street (Italianate, circa 1871) and both of the aforementioned Garth mansions.

Many of Hannibal's restored mansions and mini mansions are now private homes, including W.B. Pettibone's Cliffside Mansion (designed by Howard Van Doren Shaw, 1912), the Joseph Rowe House at 306 North Sixth Street (Second Empire, circa 1885), the Doyle-Mounce House on Maple Avenue (Second Empire, 1880) and the Sumner T. McKnight House at 1001 Bird Street (Italianate/Eastlake, 1877).

MARION COUNTY HISTORICAL SOCIETY

Another great contributor to historic preservation is the Marion County Historical Society (MCHS), organized in June 1956 with Kate Ray Kuhn as its first president. Members who were interested in preserving historic properties, as well as archives and artifacts of Marion County, came together to form the society and immediately assumed a leadership role in saving some of Hannibal's most historic buildings.

One such structure was a small stone house located at 517 Mark Twain Avenue. It was thought to have been originally built prior to 1839. The building had served many different functions over the years, including as an armory for the Union army during the Civil War, as a saloon, as a residence and as the site of the first soda water factory in Hannibal. When a plan to expand Highway 36 (Mark Twain Avenue) commenced in 1957, several homes along the south side of the street were auctioned for demolition. Marion County Historical Society members bought the old house, now known as the Welshman's House. Volunteers dismantled the house stone by stone, numbering each stone so that it could be rebuilt with accuracy. The Hannibal Women's Club donated $1,700 to MCHS in 1958 for the restoration. The City of Hannibal allowed the home to be rebuilt on city

The circa 1839 Welshman's House was disassembled and moved in 1957–58 by the Marion County Historical Society to prevent its demolition. *Courtesy Steve Chou.*

property at 509 North Third Street, and when completed, MCHS opened the home as a museum and historical landmark. The dedication ceremony took place on July 1, 1963 (during that year's National Tom Sawyer Days). A key was presented to Mayor Harry Musgrove as special guest Mrs. Frank Klever, granddaughter of Hannibal's first mayor, James Brady, looked on.

Today, the Welshman's House is owned by the City of Hannibal, and its use is granted to MCHS. Meetings are held in the space, and the building is a repository for many important documents and artifacts relating to Marion County's history.

Another significant project tackled by the Marion County Historical Society was the restoration of the birthplace of Margaret Tobin, aka the "Unsinkable Molly Brown." Having fallen into terrible disrepair, the sixteen-by thirty-foot structure was purchased at a tax sale by Mr. and Mrs. Leo Riney and then donated to the Marion County Historical Society on September 9, 1967. It was accepted by Mrs. Kate Ray Kuhn representing the society. (The Tobin House was located on Denkler's Alley, just a few feet from where the Welshman's House was originally situated, but was farther up on the slope of the hill and therefore was left in place during the widening of Highway 36.)

Restoration of Molly Brown's birthplace required hundreds of hours of volunteer labor and materials. The MCHS proudly opened Molly Brown's Birthplace as a museum on June 28, 1970. In 1998, Terrell and Vicki Dempsey led and financed a second restoration effort to keep the structure

The Molly Brown house, circa 1967, before restoration. *Courtesy Steve Chou.*

sound. It was later donated to the City of Hannibal by the Dempseys and was open for tours under the direction of the Hannibal Convention and Visitors Bureau. At the time of this writing, another restoration effort is currently underway, spearheaded by Third Ward councilman Lou Barta.

The Marion County Historical Society continues to be active in the region. MCHS secured funding from city and state resources and developed the Maple Avenue Historic District, providing tax credits for preservation of structures in the area. In 1979, a reissue of the eleven-hundred-page-long 1884 *History of Marion County* was reprinted and made available to the public by the society; recently, a second reprint was issued. Contributions of time, money and resources are made by MCHS members to various civic and historic organizations in and around Hannibal. Every year, MCHS participates in festivals and events to raise awareness of the history of the region and to encourage others to join in preserving their local heritage.

President of the Marion County Historical Society Kate Ray Kuhn (far right) and other volunteers put the finishing touches on the newly restored Molly Brown birthplace in 1970. MCHS opened the house for tours beginning in June of that year. *Courtesy Steve Chou.*

Friends of Historic Hannibal

In the mid-1990s, a group of Hannibal "transplants" began to meet to discuss the struggles and joys experienced while restoring their historic homes. Members were either new to Hannibal or had moved away and were returning to their hometown. The Friends of Historic Hannibal (FOHH) grew from these gatherings. FOHH meets once per month in the home of one of its members, where the host gives a tour of his or her home and shares the history and restoration of the structure. Having the opportunity to peer into one of Hannibal's historic homes brings fellowship and inspiration to those interested in historic preservation.

FOHH members volunteer their time and resources to many projects and events. The group hosts a Historic Homes Tour each year to help raise funds for civic projects and organizations. FOHH also participates in festivals and celebrations, including Twain on Main in May, National Tom Sawyer Days in July and the Folklife Festival in October.

One of the most ambitious projects underway by the members of FOHH is the restoration and maintenance of Old Baptist Cemetery. Founded in 1837 and platted in 1844, Old Baptist was the original interment site of Mark Twain's father, John Marshall Clemens, and his brother, Henry Clemens. (Their bodies were moved to Mt. Olivet Cemetery in the late 1870s.) Some people claim that this is the cemetery Mark Twain was describing in *The Adventures of Tom Sawyer*, where Tom and Huck take a dead cat for a séance and witness the murder of Doc Robinson by Injun Joe. A marked slave grave can be found in this cemetery, as well as the graves of dozens of Civil War soldiers, some of whom were African American soldiers who fought for the Union.

The large cemetery was active until the time of the Civil War; during that time, the Baptist Church disbanded over conflicts between congregation members, and the cemetery was abandoned. After the war, no one claimed ownership of the cemetery, nor did anyone take responsibility for its upkeep. The cemetery fell into terrible disrepair. Eventually, the site was so overgrown that some living in Hannibal did not realize there was a cemetery at the intersection of Summer and Section Streets!

In 2002, after more than 140 years of neglect, FOHH set out to reclaim the cemetery. The property had been taken over by the City of Hannibal in 1965 (100 years after it was abandoned). No work had been done to maintain the grounds, and no one had been buried in the cemetery since 1953. FOHH cleared away debris, weeds, felled trees and decades of overgrowth. Headstones were cleaned, repaired and reset. After restoring the cemetery to a manageable level by FOHH, regular maintenance of the grounds was resumed by the city. FOHH continues to restore the cemetery, and each September the FOHH picnic is held at Old Baptist amongst the gravestones.

PROMINENT HANNIBALIANS

JAKE "EAGLE EYE" BECKLEY

Among the pre-1900 and dead-ball-era players enshrined in Cooperstown, New York's Baseball Hall of Fame, Jake Beckley stands shoulder to shoulder with Ty Cobb, Honus Wagner and Cy Young, yet few baseball fans have heard of the Hannibal-born and raised first baseman who played for twenty seasons between four National League teams.

Born on August 4, 1867, Beckley worked in a local machine shop as a teenager while spending his off hours playing as a second baseman for several semiprofessional teams in and around Hannibal. A former Hannibal Blues teammate, Bob Hart, had been pitching for a Leavenworth, Kansas professional team in the Western League in 1886, and Hart recommended Beckley to the team's manager. On what would now be considered a minor-league team, the eighteen-year-old batted .342 as a left-handed second baseman and outfielder in his first season.

Because his throwing arm had proven to be weak in these positions, he was converted to a first baseman in his second season. The change benefited him, as he hit a combined .420 for Leavenworth and another Western League team in Lincoln, Nebraska, the following season. The Lincoln team then sold him to the St. Louis Whites of the Western Association (another higher-quality minor-league team) at the beginning of the 1888 season.

Jake Beckley during his period playing for the Pittsburgh Alleghenys/ Pirates of the National League from 1888 to 1896. *Courtesy John Horne/ Baseball Hall of Fame.*

It was in St. Louis where Beckley received his big break. By mid-June, he was leading the team in hitting as a twenty-year-old (.319) when he and a teammate were sold to the Pittsburgh Alleghenys of the National League for $4,500; reportedly, Beckley's price was $4,000 alone (roughly equivalent to $95,000 in 2010). Pittsburgh was fortunate in obtaining the two, for days later the Whites would disband due to insolvency. The players were bought before they could become free agents.

Beckley filled the Alleghenys' need for an everyday first baseman by batting .343 as a rookie and earning the nickname "Eagle Eye" for his hitting skills. He would play for the Alleghenys (renamed the Pirates in 1891) for seven seasons, becoming the most popular player on the team. His National League career was interrupted in 1890 when he chose to defect with eight other teammates to the newly formed Pittsburgh team of the Players' League, which was created as a response to low wages and unfair treatment of players in the National League and, to a lesser extent, the

American Association. Beckley led the Players' League in triples (twenty-two) that year before the league folded, sending him and his teammates back to the Alleghenys.

Even with a severe batting slump in 1892 following the sudden death of his new wife, Molly, Beckley achieved a .300 batting average in 930 games with Pittsburgh, leading the league in putouts three times and in assists four times. Five times he drove in at least ninety-six runs, a difficult feat in an era where home runs were scarce and one baseball would be used for the entire game or until it unraveled, making hitting conditions worse in the later innings. However, he had been in a slump in 1896, and the team decided to trade him to the New York Giants for another player and $1,000 in cash—a move that angered Pittsburgh fans.

The stint with New York lasted for the second half of 1896 and the first month of the 1897 season, with Beckley continuing his slump. Thinking Beckley's career was nearly over, the Giants released him in May, only for him to be signed within weeks by the Cincinnati Reds. The Reds needed a first baseman, and Beckley regained his stroke. His "comeback" that year culminated in a three-home-run game against the St. Louis Cardinals on September 26; no previous Reds player had ever hit three homers in a game, and no other major-league player would duplicate this feat for another twenty-five years. Beckley would play seven seasons in Cincinnati, and his .325 average ranks as the third best in Reds history.

It was during his stint for the Reds that Beckley's career nearly ended on May 8, 1901, when fellow Hall of Famer Christy Mathewson struck him in the head with a fastball. According to newspaper reports, Beckley lay unconscious for more than five minutes; remarkably, he missed only two games and finished the season with a .307 average.

Although Beckley had been performing at the highest level offensively and defensively well into his mid-thirties, the player-manager of the Reds (who wanted to play first base) sold him to the St. Louis Cardinals prior to the start of the 1904 season. His first two years with the Cardinals showed little erosion of his playing ability, but injuries forced him to miss over a third of the 1906 season. His recovery sputtered at the start of 1907, and the Cardinals released him after thirty-two games. Three months shy of his fortieth birthday, Beckley found an opening with Kansas City in the American Association; he would play three seasons there, doubling duty as a player-manager in 1909.

Baseball was such a driving force in Beckley's life that he continued to play in semiprofessional leagues after his pro career ended. In 1911, his last year as a professional player at any level, he returned to Hannibal and hit .282 as a first baseman/manager for the Hannibal Cannibals team at the age of forty-four. As late as 1913, after moving back to Kansas City, he even worked a season as an umpire for the fledgling Federal League, which would assert itself as a third major league the following year. His major league totals would impress in any era, much more so for a player from a period with some of the lowest average run scores in baseball history:

BA	G	AB	R	H	2B	3B	HR	RBI	SB
.308	2,386	9,527	1,602	2,934	473	244	88	1,578	315

More details of his totals are included below. In short, he finished his career highly ranked in several categories (rankings are based on all major-league players through the end of the 2010 season):

Number of fielding chances: most in history (25,720)
Putouts: most in history and most among first basemen (23,731)
Games played at first base: second in history (2,380) behind Eddie Murray of the Baltimore Orioles; Beckley held the record until 1994
Assists as a first baseman: 1,316, ranked eighteenth
Times hit by a pitch: 183, ranked tenth
Hits: 2,934, ranked thirty-second
Runs scored: 1,602, ranked forty-fifth
Runs batted in: 1,578, ranked thirty-ninth
Triples: 244, ranked fourth
Singles: 2,130, ranked thirtieth

Beckley operated a grain business near Kansas City after his retirement from baseball. Due to a weak heart, his retirement was cut short; he died on June 25, 1918, at fifty-one years of age.

With Beckley's longevity, consistently high levels of performance and career numbers, one could see how he would appear to be almost a lock for the Hall of Fame. Yet it wasn't until 1971—fifty-three years after his death—that the Hall's Veterans Committee voted him for inclusion, even though none of the voters had ever seen him play. How could he have been overlooked for so long?

First, he never played for a pennant-winning team, which would have given his achievements greater impact. Second, he played in parts of the pre-history and dead-ball eras, where the style of play and emphasis on statistics differed significantly from the modern era. Third, he came from a time period where media coverage was limited, even in daily newspapers, and overall attendance for an average National League team like Pittsburgh would hover around two thousand people per game at best. The game's popularity as a professional sport was still being established.

The dead-ball era has been portrayed by various biographies and histories as a lively, colorful time with intense players who would look for any advantage for the sake of winning, and Jake Beckley fits the description. The following are anecdotes culled from various newspapers and baseball histories that give a more rounded impression of his personality:

> *Beckley did not have a good arm, and his inability to make accurate throws caused one of the strangest plays ever seen in baseball. With Beckley's Cardinals (after his Reds days) playing Pittsburgh, Pirate Tommy Leach laid down a bunt along the first-base line and took off. In swooped Beckley, who fielded the ball smartly, spun, and threw in the general direction of pitcher Jack Taylor, who was covering first. The throw would have been perfect had Taylor been nine feet tall. Leach rounded first and headed for second while the ball bounded into foul territory. To redeem himself, Beckley chased the ball down and, when he saw Leach head for third under a full head of steam, charged for the plate. The crowd cheered as the two players raced home. As Leach slid feet first from one direction, Beckley made a headlong dive from the other. Leach was out and also suffered two broken ribs.*
>
> —Baseball: The Biographical History

> *Jake Beckley wasn't afraid to bend the rules. Despite his stocky build (he stood 5'10" and weighed 200 lbs.), he ran well enough to reach double figures in stolen bases and triples almost every year, but he also didn't mind cutting across the infield if the umpire's back was turned. One day, when umpire Tim Hurst wasn't looking, Jake ran almost directly from second base to home, sliding in without a throw. Hurst called Beckley out anyway. "You big son of a bitch," shouted Hurst, "you got here too fast!"*
>
> —*David Fleitz,* The Baseball Biography Project

Some of the Hannibalian's antics intended to entertain the audience while gaining a psychological advantage in the field, especially in trying to compensate for his lackluster arm strength. According to several sources, Beckley had developed a hidden ball trick to trap runners from stealing bases. He would hide the ball under a corner of the first base bag when the runner wasn't looking; when the runner would take a lead, Beckley would quickly pull the ball from under the bag and tag the runner. This worked well with rookies and players who had not faced Beckley before. Sometimes, as with Honus Wagner, Beckley would bring an extra ball into play and intentionally show he was trying to hide the ball under his armpit. Wagner grabbed the ball when the umpire's back was turned and threw the ball into the outfield, then sped off for second base. What Wagner did not know was that the actual game ball was with the pitcher, who threw the runner out with ease.

Some of Beckley's techniques influenced future team strategy and rule changes. New York Yankees managing legend Casey Stengel used Beckley's unorthodox bunting method as an example for his early teams. Just as the pitcher would finish his delivery to the plate, Beckley would flip the end of the bat and bunt using only the handle. A little too effective, the method was eventually outlawed. In addition, he would disrupt a pitcher's rhythm by yelling phrases like "Chickazoola!" while at the plate.

If it appears that Jake Beckley played an unethical brand of baseball by today's standards, his efforts reflected a general approach to the game shared by most of the successful players of the time—that of intense, aggressive competition in a game where all the rules (written and "unwritten") had not been developed yet. The emphasis in this era was placed primarily on defense and avoiding the strikeout; strategy fueled a game dominated by base hits, sacrifice bunts and stolen bases, or what would be termed "small ball" in today's language. The difficulty in fielding hits with thin, fingerless gloves was matched with the challenges of a batter facing a pitcher only forty-five feet from home plate wielding then-legal spitballs. While batters hit for average, run scoring was at a premium, and a little extra aggression or toughness could make the difference between an average player and a great one. Jake Beckley, one of the most prolific first basemen in baseball history, helped form the character and work ethic that defined the sport at the turn of the twentieth century.

James Carroll Beckwith

Carroll Beckwith, as he preferred to be known, was born in his parents' home at 400 North Fourth Street in Hannibal on September 23, 1852, the son of N.M. Beckwith. Prior to the outbreak of the Civil War, the Beckwith family moved to Chicago; soon after, Carroll's father was appointed as the United States commissioner general of the Paris Exposition of 1867.

In 1868, Beckwith began to study art at the Chicago Academy of Design. His time was cut short by the devastating Chicago Fire of 1871. Beckwith relocated to New York and resumed studies with Lemuel Wilmarth at the National Academy of Design. In November 1873, Beckwith traveled to Paris, where he continued to study. Certainly, the French Impressionists of the time had a great influence on his work, as he became known as one of the premier American painters of impressionism.

In 1877, one of his mentors, Carolus Duran, selected Beckwith and John Singer Sargent to work on a mural for the Palais du Luxembourg. Upon his marriage to Bertha Hall on June 1, 1887, Sargent presented the happy couple with a Venetian watercolor as a wedding present.

Beckwith returned to the United States in 1878. Immediately upon his arrival, he began to teach at the Art Students League of New York. He was active in both the Fine Arts Society and the National Free Art League, of which he was elected president.

As an artist, he gained prominence through his work on portraits; subjects included Mark Twain, Theodore Roosevelt and William Merritt Chase. He was awarded an Honorable Mention at the Paris Exposition of 1889 and a Gold Medal at the Atlanta Exposition of 1895 and received notoriety for his most celebrated work, a portrait of William M. Walton, at the Exposition Universelle in Paris in 1899. Another gold medal was won at the Charleston Exposition in 1902. Beckwith's painting *The Nautilus* was shown at the 1904 World's Fair in St. Louis.

Beckwith moved to Italy in 1910 and began to focus on painting en plein-air, favoring the study of monuments, buildings and landscapes. He returned to New York in 1914. After taking a cab ride through Central Park with his wife, Bertha, Beckwith died of a heart attack in their apartment on West Forty-fifth Street. He was sixty-six years old.

Carroll Beckwith bequeathed his papers, including the sketchbooks and journals he kept from 1871 until his death in 1917, to the National Academy of Design in New York City. In 1922, George A. Mahan of Hannibal donated an original Beckwith painting, the portrait of the African explorer Paul du Chailiu (a personal friend of Beckwith), to the Hannibal Public Library.

MARGARET TOBIN BROWN

On July 18, 1867, John and Johanna Tobin welcomed a daughter into the world. They named her Margaret, but the babe would come to be known by family and friends as "Maggie."

This was the second marriage for Maggie's parents, both of whom had been widowed early in life. Both had a daughter from their first marriage, Maggie's half sisters Catherine and Mary Ann. Both were born in Ireland and had immigrated to the United States during the great potato famine of the 1840s. Separately, they arrived in Hannibal before the outset of the Civil War. The Irish Catholic community in Hannibal was a tightknit group, and soon John and Johanna were acquainted. After they married and began a new family with their daughters, the couple added a son, Daniel, in 1863. Maggie was the fourth sibling and would be followed by brother William in 1869 and sister Helen in 1871.

The Tobin family lived in a small cottage that hugged the side of a steep slope on Denkler's Alley, just a few hundred feet from the Mississippi River. Their home was small and sparsely furnished. John, who worked as a laborer for the Hannibal Gas Works, earned a modest income to care for his large family.

Maggie and her siblings were educated at the home of their aunt, Mary O'Leary. Mrs. O'Leary's grammar school, just across the street on Prospect Avenue, was where many of the Irish children in the neighborhood would attend school. By all accounts, Maggie had a happy childhood. She was close to her siblings and her cousins and part of a supportive local Irish community.

Her childhood years, the years during Reconstruction, were also some of the most prosperous years for Hannibal. Maggie would witness the opening of the first bridge across the Mississippi in Hannibal, the first streetcars and the advent of telephone service. Railroads and riverboats added to the excitement of the ebb and flow of life in the bustling port city.

After graduating from Mary O'Leary's grammar school, thirteen-year-old Maggie was expected to contribute to the family's coffers. Maggie took a job working for the D.J. Garth & Brothers Tobacco Company, which processed more than a half million pounds of tobacco per year. Most likely, Maggie was assigned, as most women were at the plant, to strip the leaves of their stems to prepare for manufacturing plug, twist, chewing and smoking tobacco. (Only men were given the high-paying jobs of rolling cigars, some making as much as two dollars per day.)

Maggie also worked as a waitress at the Continental Hotel's dining room on Center Street in the alley between Third and Fourth Streets. She is rumored to have also served in that capacity at the luxurious Park Hotel, at Fourth and Center, which opened in 1880. Legend has it that she met Mark Twain while working at the Park Hotel, where he told her of the riches of the mines in Colorado, but most Twain and Brown scholars believe this is a fabrication that may have been perpetuated by Margaret Brown herself.

In 1886, Margaret boarded a train at Hannibal's new Union Depot bound for Denver, Colorado. She had been beckoned to Colorado by her half sister Mary Ann and brother Daniel, both of whom had settled in Leadville, a mining community. Margaret took a job at the Daniels, Fisher and Smith Department Store in Leadville, where she hemmed draperies and stitched carpeting. While working at the store, she met her future husband, James Joseph "J.J." Brown. They were married in September of that year and later had two children together, Larry and Catherine.

In early 1893, J.J. Brown was a supervisor working for the Ibex Mining Company when he engineered the construction of a shaft that would allow the "Little Jonny" Mine to be tapped. Gold, silver and copper ore were found inside "Little Jonny," and by October 1893, the mine was producing 135 tons of gold ore per day. For his efforts, J.J. Brown was given one-eighth ownership of the mining company and was named to the board of directors. The Browns became millionaires.

While in Leadville, Margaret first became involved in women's rights by helping to establish the Colorado chapter of the National American Women's Suffrage Association and working in soup kitchens to assist miners' families. In 1894, the Browns moved to Denver, where Margaret became a charter member of the Denver Woman's Club dedicated to the improvement of women's lives through education and philanthropy.

Margaret traveled the world and in 1912 boarded the RMS *Titanic* on its maiden voyage from Cherbourg, France. After striking an iceberg in the North Atlantic on its way to America, the ship sank. Margaret was instrumental in assisting survivors on Lifeboat Number 6, and after they boarded the rescue ship RMS *Carpathia*, Margaret took up a collection with other first-class passengers and raised more than $10,000 to donate to the newly widowed women and orphaned children who had survived the disaster. It was this experience that garnered Margaret the nickname "Unsinkable."

Taking advantage of the fame she earned as a heroine of the *Titanic* disaster, Margaret began to bring awareness to issues she championed. She was involved with the National Women's Trade Union League, which called for a federal minimum wage and eight-hour workdays. She joined Alice Paul and worked for the National Woman's Suffrage Association to give women the right to vote, and she was one of the organizers of the Conference of Great Women. Because of her leadership qualities, supporters encouraged Margaret to run for a seat in the U.S. Senate in 1914, but her nomination did not progress into election.

Margaret turned her attention to the war in Europe and made her way to France. During World War I, she volunteered in military hospitals caring for injured soldiers. After the war, Margaret assisted the American Committee for Devastated France, rebuilding areas that had been behind the front lines. For her efforts, Margaret was awarded the French Legion of Honor.

In her later years, Margaret aspired to be an actress and appeared in a production of *L'Aiglon* in both New York and Paris, recreating the role made famous by Sandra Bernhardt. While living at the famed Barbizon Hotel for actresses, Margaret died in New York City on October 26, 1932, of a brain tumor and cerebral hemorrhage at the age of sixty-five. She is buried in the Cemetery of Holy Rood in Westbury, New York.

Margaret Brown was never known as "Molly" during her lifetime. This nickname was assigned when Margaret was immortalized in the 1960 Broadway production of *The Unsinkable Molly Brown*, starring Tammy Grimes (who won the Tony Award for her performance). Debbie Reynolds portrayed Molly Brown in the movie version in 1964. James Cameron's 1997 film *Titanic* revived interest in Margaret Brown once again. These characterizations have added to the myths and legends surrounding the amazing life of Margaret Brown, the young Irish lass from Hannibal, Missouri.

BLANCHE KELSO BRUCE

Born a slave in Mississippi on March 1, 1841, Blanche Kelso Bruce was the son of Pettis Perkinson, a white plantation owner in Virginia, and an African American house slave named Polly Bruce. Bruce's father took special interest in him and allowed him to be educated with his legitimate white half brother. Eventually, Bruce was legally emancipated by his father, who also arranged for Bruce to begin to serve as an apprentice in a printer's office.

Bruce moved to Missouri and continued his apprenticeship. When the Civil War broke out, Bruce volunteered to fight for the Union army; because of his race, he was rejected. Instead, Bruce spent the war years attending Oberlin College in Ohio.

After the war, Bruce was employed as a porter on a Mississippi River steamboat. He was thus introduced to the bustling, diverse community of Hannibal, where he decided to make his home. It was during this period that Bruce began to teach at the first school for African Americans in Hannibal.

The Baptist Church, founded in 1853 by the Reverend Oliver S. Webb, was located at Eighth and Center Streets. The one-room sanctuary was used as a church on Sundays and, after Emancipation, as the first school for Hannibal's black population during the week. Reverend Thomas Henderson was the school's first instructor, teaching both African American adults and children. In 1864, Bruce would assume Reverend Henderson's duties as instructor.

During the years of Reconstruction, Bruce became a wealthy landowner in the Mississippi Delta. He won election as sheriff in Bolivar County, Mississippi, and was later also elected as tax collector and supervisor of education. In 1874, Bruce was elected to Congress as a Republican senator from Mississippi. He was the first African American, and the only former slave, to serve a full six-year term in the U.S. Senate.

At the 1880 Republican National Convention in Chicago, Bruce won eight votes for vice president, giving him the distinction of being the first African American to win votes in a major party's nominating convention. He was appointed by President James Garfield to be the register of the United States Treasury, making Bruce the first African American whose signature appeared on United States paper currency.

Blanche Kelso Bruce died in Washington, D.C., in 1898. His house, located at 909 M Street Northwest, was declared a National Historic Landmark in 1975.

MARIE ROUFF BYRUM

Early in the morning on August 31, 1920, rain was falling in Hannibal. A determined twenty-six-year-old woman set out to walk fifteen muddy blocks. She was on a very special mission. Accompanying her was her husband, Morris Byrum, Hannibal's city clerk.

When the couple reached their destination, they were met by Morris's father, Lacey Byrum. A special election was being held that day, and Lacey Byrum was serving as the Democratic election judge. It was his suggestion that Marie Rouff Byrum appear at the polling place by 7:00 a.m. to cast her ballot. The election was being held to fill a vacancy on the Hannibal City Council.

As Marie slipped her vote into the ballot box, she became the very first woman to vote in the United States. The passage of the Nineteenth Amendment to the United States Constitution had been ratified just five days earlier. Her vote fulfilled the dreams of women suffragists across the country and ushered in a new chapter of American history.

SAMUEL LANGHORNE CLEMENS

In 1835, people around the world witnessed the arrival of a bright "star." As Halley's comet passed through the sky above, Samuel Langhorne Clemens was born on a small farm in Florida, Missouri, on November 30, 1835. Sammy was the sixth of seven children born to John Marshall Clemens and his wife, Jane. In 1839, when Sammy was just four years old, John Marshall Clemens began to hear stories of opportunity and prosperity found in the port city of Hannibal, just thirty miles east. He moved his family to Hannibal and set up shop, operating a general store near the intersection of Main and Hill Streets.

Although the Clemens family always struggled financially, Sam enjoyed an exciting, adventurous childhood in Hannibal. The Mississippi River was his playground, the caves were his hideout, and Sam had a large band of neighborhood children to entertain. Sam Clemens's memories of childhood, both happy and bittersweet, would be recalled time and again in his voluminous writings as Mark Twain, most notably in the American classic, *The Adventures of Tom Sawyer*.

John Marshall Clemens died in 1847. Sam, only eleven years old, was expected to contribute to the household. He soon became an apprentice in the offices of the *Missouri Courier*, where he learned to set type. Later, his older brother Orion would own a newspaper in Hannibal, and it was here that Sam Clemens had the first opportunity to try his hand at writing.

In the summer of 1853, Sam Clemens left Hannibal to seek his fortune in life. For the next several years, he traveled to St. Louis, New York, Philadelphia and Washington, D.C., working odd jobs at various newspapers. By 1857, he fulfilled a childhood dream, becoming an apprentice pilot on the steamboat *Paul Jones*. Sam would eventually earn his pilot's license and enjoy several years traveling up and down the Mississippi River until the outbreak of the Civil War in 1861 brought his riverboat days to an end.

During the 1860s, Sam ventured west, dabbling in mining and occasionally writing for newspapers. The first use of his famous pen name, Mark Twain, came in 1863 while writing for the *Territorial Enterprise* in Virginia City, Nevada. Clemens borrowed the name from his days as a riverboat pilot: the term "Mark Twain" means "two fathoms" or twelve feet, the minimum depth required on the Mississippi River for safe navigation by a steamboat.

In 1865, Mark Twain recorded the written version of a story he'd heard while traveling by stagecoach through Nevada and California. The tale, "Jim Smiley and his Jumping Frog," was published by the New York weekly the *Saturday Press* on November 18, 1865. The popularity of the tall tale brought national attention to Twain's writing. (The story would be renamed "The Celebrated Jumping Frog of Calaveras County" when published again in 1867.)

Twain's humor and wit attracted the attention of the *Sacramento* [California] *Union*, which sent him on an excursion to the Sandwich Islands (present-day Hawaii). This would become the first of many trips abroad, each providing fodder for travelogues Twain would write for publication. Upon his return, Twain would also use these experiences to speak on the lecture circuit, telling colorful and humorous tales about the places he traveled and the people he met along the way.

While on a trip to Europe in 1867, Twain befriended Charles Langdon, son of a wealthy family in New York. Legend has it that Langdon showed a picture of his sister Olivia to Twain; later, Twain claimed to have fallen in love with her at first sight of the photograph. Upon their return to the United States, Langdon introduced Twain to Olivia in 1868. The couple was engaged a year later and married on February 2, 1870, in Elmira, New York. They would have three daughters together: Suzy, born in 1872; Clara, born in 1874; and Jean, born in 1880. A son, Langdon, died in his infancy in 1872.

The Clemens family lived in a beautiful home in Hartford, Connecticut. It is here that Mark Twain wrote many of his best-known works, including *The Adventures of Tom Sawyer* (1876), *The Prince and the Pauper* (1881), *Life on the Mississippi* (1883), *Adventures of Huckleberry Finn* (1884) and *A Connecticut Yankee in King Arthur's Court* (1889).

Although he achieved great success as a writer and public speaker, Mark Twain was a poor businessman. He loved science and technology and invested heavily in several inventions, none of which would bring any financial gain. His business losses soon led him to bankruptcy, but even after legally being relieved of his debts, Mark Twain continued to travel, write and lecture, determined to pay each of his creditors in full.

In the spring of 1902, Mark Twain was to receive an honorary doctorate from the University of Missouri in Columbia. Traveling by train, Twain decided to make an unplanned stop in Hannibal. It would be his final visit to his boyhood hometown and proved to be a very moving experience.

Twain would outlive nearly all whom he loved. Daughter Suzy contracted meningitis and died in 1896. Twain's beloved wife, Olivia, passed away while the couple was living in Italy in 1904. Jean, Twain's youngest daughter, who suffered from epilepsy, drowned in her bathtub on Christmas Eve 1909.

"I came in with Halley's Comet in 1835," Twain told his biographer in 1909.

> *It is coming again next year, and I expect to go out with it. It will be the greatest disappointment of my life if I don't go out with Halley's Comet. The Almighty has said, no doubt: "Now here are these two unaccountable freaks; they came in together, they must go out together."*

His wish was fulfilled. Mark Twain died from a heart attack on April 21, 1910, just one day after Halley's comet made its closest approach to Earth. He was seventy-four years old.

When President William Howard Taft learned of Twain's death, he said:

> *Mark Twain gave pleasure—real intellectual enjoyment—to millions, and his works will continue to give such pleasure to millions yet to come...*

His humor was American, but he was nearly as much appreciated by Englishmen and people of other countries as by his own countrymen. He has made an enduring part of American literature.

Throughout the twentieth century, Twain's books would be published in nearly every country and every language on the planet. *The Adventures of Tom Sawyer* has, to date, never been out of print since first released in 1876. Twain is regularly lauded as one of the greatest authors of American literature and continues to be popular more than one hundred years after his death.

Twain's last work was his autobiography, which he dictated to hired stenographers during the last several years of his life. He believed that it would be more entertaining if he spoke of recollections as they came to him rather than trying to recall the events of his life in chronological order. Unfortunately, after his death, editors took the thousands of pages of transcripts and rearranged the biography into more conventional forms, ignoring Twain's own ideas of how to present the material.

The year 2010 marked the 100th anniversary of Twain's death, and in November 2010, the University of California Press (Berkeley) released the first of three volumes of Mark Twain's newly restored autobiography, unexpurgated. The editors took great care to present the information as closely to Twain's original intent as possible. The first volume contains more than 700 pages. Thinking that it would only appeal to hard-core Twain scholars, only ten thousand copies were ordered for the first printing. To the editors' surprise, the book quickly shot up the *New York Times* bestseller list, where it remains in the top ten at the time of this writing, selling more than a half million copies in its first four months of release. Twain now has the distinction of being one of only a handful of authors to have bestselling publications in the nineteenth, twentieth and twenty-first centuries.

ROBERT E. COONTZ

On June 11, 1864, Robert E. Coontz was born to Mr. and Mrs. Benton Coontz in their home at 303 North Sixth Street in Hannibal. Benton Coontz was a prominent business and civic leader in Hannibal who, in 1880, assumed ownership of Hannibal's horse-drawn streetcar system. Fourteen-year-old Robert learned to drive the streetcars by taking over during the regular drivers' lunch hours and breaks; soon, he was promoted to conductor, and by the age of fifteen, he became superintendent of the railway.

While working for his father's streetcar service, Coontz also attended Hannibal College. During this period, William Henry Hatch, the U.S. congressman from Hannibal, visited the Coontz family. Robert took the opportunity to ask Hatch for an appointment to the U.S. Naval Academy in Annapolis. Several other Hannibal boys had inquired, as well; so, to choose who would receive his support, Hatch gave the boys a "competitive examination." Coontz was the victor.

Robert Coontz graduated from the U.S. Naval Academy in 1885. For the next decade, Coontz served in the navy, stationed on vessels in Alaska and the Great Lakes. He was assigned to the Office of the Department of Navy in 1894 and was later reassigned to the cruiser USS *Philadelphia*. While aboard the USS *Charleston*, Coontz was sent to the Pacific and saw action in the Spanish-American War.

From December 17, 1907, to February 22, 1909, Coontz, now a lieutenant commander, participated in what came to be known as "The Great White Fleet." President Theodore Roosevelt, nearing the end of his administration, ordered sixteen battleships and various escort ships to commence on a worldwide voyage in an effort to demonstrate American military power at sea. All ships had their hulls painted white, the navy's peacetime color scheme. The Great White Fleet was greeted by cheering crowds in places such as Sydney, Australia; Yokohama, Japan; and Messina, Sicily. The fleet would set numerous world

Admiral Robert E. Coontz. *Courtesy Library of Congress.*

records, including one for the incredible number of ships simultaneously circumnavigating the earth. Coontz was named executive officer of the battleship USS *Nebraska* during the expedition.

After completion of the highly successful voyage of the Great White Fleet, Coontz was promoted to the rank of commander and assigned to the U.S. Naval Academy, where he served as commandant of midshipmen. In 1912, he served as governor of Guam and commanding officer of the battleship USS *Georgia*. In 1918, he was commandant of the Puget Sound Navy Yard and the Thirteenth Naval District.

Promoted to the rank of rear admiral, Coontz assumed command of an entire battleship division in the Atlantic. In 1919, he had just been assigned to the Pacific Fleet when he was selected to succeed Admiral William S. Benson as chief of naval operations (CNO). While dealing with the politics of this elevated position, Coontz established a unified United States Fleet and strengthened the position of CNO within the Navy Department.

In 1923, Admiral Coontz returned to the sea as commander in chief of the U.S. Fleet. He returned to the rank of rear admiral in 1925 to serve as commandant of the Fifth Naval District. After forty-seven years of service, Coontz retired from the navy in June 1928.

Admiral Coontz's memoir of his naval career, *From the Mississippi to the Sea*, was published in 1930. Five years later, on January 26, 1935, he died at the Naval Hospital in Puget Sound, Washington, at the age of seventy-one. Upon his wishes, he was brought back to Hannibal for burial and a full military funeral was arranged. The cortege, which included a horse-drawn wagon carrying the admiral's body, was observed by hundreds of onlookers as it made its way through the streets of Hannibal to Admiral Coontz's final resting place at Mount Olivet Cemetery.

The United States Navy would honor Admiral Coontz by naming two ships in his honor, the USS *Coontz* and the USS *Admiral R.E. Coontz*.

In 1938, the Works Progress Administration was assigned to construct an armory in Hannibal next to Clemens Field (another WPA project). The massive structure, which cost an estimated $175,000 at the time, was dedicated on November 5, 1939, and named in honor of Admiral Coontz. Performing at the ceremony that evening was the Harry James Band, featuring a young singer named Frank Sinatra.

CLIFTON A. EDWARDS

Cliff Edwards was born in Hannibal on June 14, 1895, in a houseboat at the foot of Church Street to Edward and Nellie Edwards. When he was quite young, his father, a railroad worker, became too ill to work, and young Clifton sold newspapers to help support his family. When he was ten years old, he began to work at the Roberts, Johnson and Rand shoe company in Hannibal. He was employed there for several years; some co-workers later reported that he would sing as he worked, entertaining the other laborers.

By age fourteen, he was ready to break away and traveled south to St. Louis. There, Edwards found work singing in saloons. Lillian McIntyre, who managed several moving picture houses and vaudeville theaters in St. Louis, hired Edwards to sing accompaniments to illustrated songs projected by "magic lantern" slides. He taught himself to play the ukulele (the least expensive instrument to buy) and, with Ms. McIntyre's encouragement, began to perform in vaudeville. Edwards made the rounds on the vaudeville circuit, eventually making it to the Arsonia Café in Chicago, Illinois. Edwards would sing and strum his ukulele from table to table to earn tips. Spot, a waiter at the Arsonia, could never remember Edwards's name and took to calling him "Ike." The nickname stuck.

At the Arsonia, "Ukulele Ike" performed a tune called "Ja Da," written by the club's pianist, Bob Carleton. Edwards and Carleton made the tune a hit on the vaudeville circuit. Vaudeville headliner Joe Frisco hired Edwards as part of his act, which was featured at the Palace in New York City, the most prestigious theater in vaudeville. The Ziegfeld Follies came next, and Edwards's career skyrocketed in 1924, when he appeared in George Gershwin's *Lady Be Good* on Broadway with Fred and Adele Astaire, stealing the show with his rendition of Gershwin's "Fascinatin' Rhythm."

Edwards made his first phonograph records in 1919 and recorded early examples of jazz scat singing in 1922. The following year, he signed a contract with Pathé Records. He became one of the most popular singers of the decade, recording many of the pop and novelty hits of the day, including "California, Here I Come," "Hard Hearted Hannah," "Yes Sir, That's My Baby," "Toot, Toot, Tootsie! (Goo'bye!)," "It Had to Be You" and "I'll See You in My Dreams." It is rumored that Edwards earned as much as $1,000 to record each song, plus three-cent royalties on each copy of records sold.

In 1925, his recording of "Paddlin' Madeleine Home" would reach number three on the pop charts. His recording of "I Can't Give You Anything But Love" was number one on the U.S. pop singles chart in 1928. The first recording of "Singin' in the Rain" was made famous by Edwards and reached number one on the charts for three weeks in 1929. He also recorded a few "off-color" novelty numbers for under-the-counter sales, including "I'm a Bear in a Lady's Boudoir" and "Who Takes Care of the Caretakers Daughter (While the Caretakers Busy Taking Care)." His recordings would go on to sell more than 74 million copies between 1923 and 1933.

More than any other performer, Edwards was responsible for the soaring popularity of the ukulele in the 1920s. Millions of ukes were sold during the decade, and Tin Pan Alley publishers added ukulele chords to standard sheet music.

Cliff Edwards made it to Hollywood in the 1920s. In 1929, Edwards was playing at the Orpheum Theater in Los Angeles, California, where he caught the attention of movie producer/director Irving Thalberg. His film company, Metro-Goldwyn-Mayer (MGM), hired Edwards to appear in early sound movies. After performing in some short films, Edwards was one of the stars in the feature *Hollywood Revue of 1929*, doing some comic bits and singing, including the film debut of his hit "Singin' in the Rain." He appeared in twenty-three films for MGM between 1929 and 1933.

MGM's comedy star Buster Keaton and Edwards became good friends, and the pair appeared together in three films. Keaton, himself a former vaudevillian, enjoyed singing and would harmonize with Edwards between takes. One of these casual jam sessions was captured on film in the 1930 *Doughboys*, in which Buster and Cliff scat-sing their way through "You Never Did That Before."

Edwards appeared in fifty-four movies during the 1930s, sharing the screen with stars such as Joan Crawford, John Gilbert, Clark Gable, Marion Davies, Robert Montgomery, Barbara Stanwyck, Helen Hayes, Rosalind Russell, Spencer Tracy, Jean Harlow, Cary Grant and Ronald Reagan. He was cast as Endicott in the screwball comedy film *His Girl Friday* and the Reminiscent Soldier in *Gone with the Wind* with Vivien Leigh and Olivia De Havilland (the scene shows the characters casting large shadows on a church wall; in movie stills, Edwards can be seen, but the final cut of the movie features his character in voice only).

In 1940 came his most famous voice role as Jiminy Cricket in Walt Disney's *Pinocchio*. Edwards's touching rendition of "When You Wish Upon a Star" earned the Oscar for Best Song that year, the first won by Disney. Another Disney Film, 1941's *Dumbo*, featured Edwards as the lead crow singing "When I See an Elephant Fly." Edwards would appear in more than one hundred films throughout his career.

In 1932, Cliff Edwards got his first national radio show on CBS. He would continue hosting popular radio shows on all four major networks through 1946.

Edwards was also a popular film cowboy "sidekick," appearing in twenty-one westerns. During 1941–42, he became the sidekick of Charles Starrett, with whom he would make eight films. Next, RKO put Edwards under contract to co-star with the Oklahoma cowboy Tim Holt. Holt had announced that he was planning to join the army to fight in World War II. RKO cranked out six western films featuring Holt and Edwards in one fifty-four-day period so as to have the films ready for individual, periodic release while Holt was overseas.

Like many vaudeville stars, Edwards was also an early arrival on television. For the 1949 season, Edwards starred in *The Cliff Edwards Show*, a TV variety show airing on Mondays, Wednesdays and Fridays on CBS.

Cliff Edwards, also known as "Ukelele Ike" and the voice of Walt Disney's Jiminy Cricket. *Courtesy Library of Congress.*

In the 1950s and early 1960s, he made a number of appearances on *The Mickey Mouse Club*, in addition to reprising his Jiminy Cricket voice for various Disney shorts and the Disney Christmas spectacular, *From All of Us to All of You.*

Edwards battled alcoholism and drug addiction for many years and suffered economic hardships throughout his career, exacerbated by having been divorced three times. By the late 1960s, he was living in a home for indigent actors and had dropped out of the public eye. At the time of his death on July 17, 1971, he was a charity patient at the Virgil Convalescent Hospital in Hollywood, California. His body was initially unclaimed and was donated to the University of California–Los Angeles medical school for research.

Hearing that no one had claimed Edwards's remains, Gary Schmedding, news director of KHMO radio in Hannibal, related the circumstances to his listeners. George Pace of the Hannibal Chamber of Commerce arranged to provide interment services with help from various Hannibal services. A nationwide news service picked up the story of Hannibal's offer of assistance, and Walt Disney Productions heard of the situation. Disney (which had been quietly paying many of Edwards's medical expenses) was able to retrieve Edwards's remains, and the Actors' Fund of America and the Motion Picture and Television Relief Fund financed the funeral services. Edwards was finally laid to rest in Valhalla Memorial Park in Los Angeles.

In 2002, Edwards's original Columbia recording of "When You Wish Upon a Star" was inducted into the Grammy Awards Hall of Fame. Edwards has also been honored by the Ukulele Society of America.

Lowell "Cotton" Fitzsimmons

Lowell Fitzsimmons was born in Hannibal on October 7, 1931. His father, a dry goods delivery driver, moved the family from town to town in northeastern Missouri, including Shelbina and Palmyra, before finally settling them in Bowling Green (thirty miles south of Hannibal).

Lowell, nicknamed "Cotton" by elementary school classmates because of his white-blond hair, lost his father at the age of eleven. His mother worked to raise her four children alone, but another figure stepped into Cotton's life: Bowling Green high school basketball coach James A. Wilson.

Wilson began to work with the seventh-grade Cotton and would mentor him throughout his high school career. Twice, Coach Wilson took his varsity high school team, which included five-foot-seven Cotton, to the Missouri State Tournament.

For two years after high school, Fitzsimmons worked at a local brick manufacturing plant to help support his family. Eventually, he began to attend Hannibal-LaGrange Junior College (HLG). He was named an all-American for HLG in 1953, his senior year, when he averaged more than twenty-five points per game. Fitzsimmons then played for Midwestern (Texas) State, where he averaged more than thirteen points per game and earned his master's degree in administrative education.

Cotton Fitzsimmons began as basketball coach for Moberly (Missouri) Junior College in 1956. In the last two of his eleven years there, Coach Fitzsimmons's team won the National Junior College Championship in 1966 and 1967. Next, he was hired by Kansas State University (KSU). He would only coach at KSU for two years before being wooed into coaching for the NBA.

In 1970, Fitzsimmons took over the reins as the Phoenix Suns head coach, taking the team to its first winning season, with a 48-34 record. He moved on to coach the Atlanta Hawks in 1972. Fitzsimmons became the player personnel director for NBA champions Golden State Warriors in 1976 and moved on to the Buffalo Braves in 1977.

After just one season with the Braves, Coach Fitzsimmons transferred to the Kansas City Kings as head coach. With the Kings in 1979, he was named the NBA's Coach of the Year.

In 1984, Fitzsimmons became the head coach of the San Antonio Spurs. He would again be named NBA Coach of the Year after returning to the Phoenix Suns in 1989.

In 1992, Fitzsimmons became the sixth coach to reach the milestone of eight hundred wins in the NBA. He retired for a short time, working as an on-air commentator, but was persuaded to return as the Suns head coach for a third time in 1996.

When he retired in 1997, Cotton Fitzsimmons had recorded 832 wins and 775 losses. He was inducted into the National Junior College Hall of Fame in 1985 and into the Missouri Sports Hall of Fame in 1988. His jersey number was also retired at Hannibal-LaGrange College.

Fitzsimmons died of a stroke while battling lung cancer on July 24, 2004. The *Arizona Republic*, in the headline of the sports section the next morning, proclaimed "Brightest Sun Fitzsimmons Dies."

WILLIAM HENRY HATCH

William H. Hatch was born in Scott County, Kentucky, on September 11, 1833. The son of a Protestant minister, Hatch was educated in Lexington and called to the bar in September 1854 at the age of twenty-one. He moved to Hannibal in 1855 and became a noted lawyer. Hatch, a member of the Democratic Party, was elected circuit attorney in 1858.

During the Civil War, Hatch fought for the Confederacy, where he served as a commissioned captain and assistant adjutant general. In March 1863, he was assigned as assistant commissioner responsible for the exchange of prisoners, a position he held until the end of the war.

Hatch returned to Hannibal in 1865 and resumed practicing law. In 1878, Hatch won election as Missouri's Twelfth District U.S. Representative. He would be reelected and serve eight consecutive terms.

In 1882, Hatch petitioned Congress for the construction of a federally funded civic building in Hannibal that would serve to house the United States District Courts and Post Office. Construction for the Federal Building

The statue of William Henry Hatch, sculpted by Frederick Hibbard, stands today in Central Park. *Photo by Ken Marks.*

was approved by an act of Congress on May 25, 1882. The site, located on Broadway between Sixth and Seventh Streets, was acquired on July 31, 1883, and construction began one year later.

Renowned architect Mifflin E. Bell, who had previously completed the Illinois and Iowa state capitol buildings, designed a magnificent Second Empire structure to be made from Bedford limestone. The building would be three stories high with a mansard roof that would add an additional level and another mansard-roofed tower at the southeast corner.

In 1885, construction on the Federal Building had been suspended at the second-floor level due to lack of funding. Bell set out to alter his design with the intent to complete the building by roofing the second floor. Hatch persuaded Bell to continue with his original plan and was able to secure four additional appropriations from Congress to finance the project. The Federal Building, complete with all three floors and its southeast tower, was dedicated in 1888. Today, the Federal Building is on the National Register of Historic Places and is the second oldest civil structure in Missouri (the first being the post office in downtown St. Louis).

"Farmer Bill" Hatch was known as a champion of agriculture. He served as chairman on the Committee on Agriculture and successfully led the movement for the creation of the cabinet position of secretary of agriculture in 1889.

Hatch's pure-food reforms included the Bureau of Animal Husbandry Act of 1884, the Oleomargarine Act of 1886 (calling for federal inspection of margarine production) and the Meat Inspection Act of 1890. He was also instrumental in the establishment of national standards for the hygienic maintenance of livestock to help control the spread of communicable animal diseases.

His greatest contribution to American agriculture was the Hatch Act of 1887. This allowed for federal funding to support agricultural experimental stations associated with land-grant colleges. The Hatch Act created more than fifty research stations, and their advancements and discoveries helped revolutionize agricultural methodologies and improve the lives of the American farmer. Further, the Office of Experimental Stations was created in the U.S. Department of Agriculture in 1888.

In 1894, after illness prohibited campaigning, Hatch was defeated for reelection to Congress. He retired to his farm west of Hannibal and died there on December 23, 1896. He is buried at Riverside Cemetery. Upon his death, it was his desire that his farm be donated to the State of Missouri for use as an agricultural experiment station.

JACK B. KUBISCH

Jack B. Kubisch was born in Hannibal on November 5, 1921. He received a bachelor of arts degree from the University of Missouri in 1942. After college, Kubisch enlisted in the U.S. Navy and served on the USS *New York* and USS *Guam* during World War II. He was in action in the Philippines and was present at the battles on Iwo Jima and Okinawa.

After the war, Kubisch was enrolled in Harvard Business School, and in 1947 he joined the United States Foreign Service. He was posted in Paris in 1949 and was the assistant to W. Averell Harriman at Marshall Plan Headquarters.

During the 1950s, Kubisch worked in the private sector but rejoined the Foreign Service in 1961. He served as director of the USAID (United States Agency for International Development) mission in Rio de Janeiro

Jack Kubisch, U.S. ambassador to Greece, 1974–77. *Courtesy Don Cullimore/Central Methodist University–Missouri.*

and, after returning to Washington, D.C., was named director of the State Department's Office of Brazilian Affairs.

In 1971, Kubish represented the United States in the Paris Peace Accords, assisting with the responsibility of negotiating the end of the Vietnam War. President Richard Nixon then named Kubish as assistant secretary of state for Inter-American Affairs, being confirmed for the post by Congress.

Kubisch was appointed by President Gerald Ford as the United States ambassador to Greece in August 1974, a position he held until September 1977. He retired to North Carolina in 1979 and died peacefully in his sleep at home on May 7, 2007.

WILLIAM P. LEAR

William Powell Lear's name has been most often associated with the business jet that bears his surname, but the jet represents only a portion of the prolific Hannibal-born inventor's influence upon the aviation and communications industries, with over 140 patents filed in his name.

Lear's achievements reflected a Horatio Alger–like rise from humble beginnings. Born on June 26, 1902, Lear suffered from a fractured home at an early age, as his parents separated when he was six years old. He moved with his mother to the South Side of Chicago, where living in poverty heavily influenced his drive to escape his surroundings. By age ten, he was inspired to start a career in electronics while listening to a report of the *Titanic* disaster on an amateur radio broadcast. Three years later, he had already built a small business by building his own battery charger and selling its services—an increasing need for the public, with battery costs running high and in demand for use in early electronic devices such as radios.

Lear had taken the initiative early in self-education, as he actively sought out whatever books and magazines were available to feed his interests in science, electronics and entrepreneurship. In a late interview, Lear confirmed that he had decided to become an inventor by age twelve:

> *I resolved first to make enough money so I'd never be stopped from finishing anything. Second, that to accumulate money in a hurry—and I was in a hurry—I'd have to invent something that people wanted, and third, that if I ever was going to stand on my own feet, I'd have to leave home.*

Lear realized that he would have to actively seek the education and training he needed; that is, learning not provided in a traditional school setting. He left school after graduating from the eighth grade and lied about his age the following year in order to join the navy. Before being honorably discharged early, he gained valuable experience as a radio technician. From there, he worked as a Western Union operator in Chicago and as a serviceman for the U.S. Air Mail at Grant Park Airport. At the latter, he managed to receive flying lessons, a harbinger of his heavy involvement with aviation technology that would consume the majority of his career.

In 1922, the twenty-year-old started his first business in nearby Quincy, Illinois, as Quincy Radio Laboratories, a radio manufacturing and repair shop. He opened the Lear Radio Laboratory in Tulsa, Oklahoma, two years later, and it was there that Lear began to make improvements on "battery eliminators," which would convert tabletop radios to accept household current. Development in the radio business was booming, and he started the Radio Coil and Wire Corporation in 1926 based in Chicago. During the next few years, he refined audio technology in attempts to make radios more portable. By 1928, he had traded the corporation to Paul Galvin to become part owner of the Galvin Manufacturing Company (which was located in the same building as Radio Coil and Wire). This last connection provided the springboard for Lear to produce a practical car radio in 1929 that could stand up to mass production.

The time frame for the invention of the first car radio has been debated, with claims that as early as 1922, several instances of tabletop radios being attached to automobiles have been documented. However, early attempts at this technology suffered from unwieldiness and lack of power or durability, and a design that could be easily duplicated had not emerged. Lear, with engineering partner Elmer Wavering, faced several obstacles in designing a mass-manufactured car radio:

> *Different electrical functions within a car would cause reception interference to the radio. In addition, Lear and Wavering would have to alter their design in order to protect against an electrical fire.*
>
> *At that time, the radio required a separate power source from the rest of the car; the battery, speaker, and receiver were to occupy space in a vehicle that was not designed to accommodate accessories.*

Many roads in America were not paved (or poorly paved); the radio needed to possess the strength to absorb the same beating the car received over a long period of time.

When Lear and Wavering installed the prototype into Galvin's Studebaker in 1930, the process took two days, with the entire dashboard being dismantled and holes driven into the ceiling and floorboard for the receiver/speaker, antenna and battery access. The car was then tested on an 850-mile journey from Chicago to Atlantic City, New Jersey, where the annual Radio Manufacturers Association Convention was being held. Lear and Wavering could not afford marketing, so the car was parked on the pier outside the convention space and demonstrated to any and all who would listen. They garnered enough sales orders from the convention to begin manufacturing what would be the first Motorola car radio. Lear named the new company from the combination of Motor(car) and Victrola. (As a side note, the original cost for the radio uninstalled was $110, while a new car ranged close to $650.)

Buoyed from his success, Lear sold the remainder of his shares in the corporation to Galvin in order to begin his first foray into aeronautic electronics, Lear, Inc. He would later improve on the cost of manufacturing radios by patenting a common "front end" that would connect to a range of different types of radios; he received $250,000 from RCA for rights and consulting fees to his "Magic Brain" radio, introduced in 1934.

However, most of Lear's work after 1931 centered on aircraft communications. After flying a biplane from Chicago to New York (which he learned to fly with two and a half hours of instruction), he realized the difficulty of navigating a plane using only a compass and landmarks. His first idea was to develop an aircraft-dedicated radio direction finder based on beacon signals. This resulted in the Lear-O-Matic finder, which earned him the Frank M. Hawks Memorial award for achievement in aviation.

Lear's forte was in taking new technologies in still-developing fields and recombining them to fill gaps in these growing markets. For example, the idea for an airplane autopilot originated in the mid-1910s with a gyroscope-based model that worked from a pilot-programmed compass. Throughout the 1940s, Lear's World War II contracts with the U.S. government (servicing over $100 million in orders) enabled him to invest in creating a lightweight electronics-based autopilot system that could automatically land an airplane

William Lear demonstrating his Lear-o-Scope, an autopilot gage that followed radio beacon signals. *Courtesy Library of Congress.*

in "zero-zero," or zero-visibility, weather. For this achievement, President Harry Truman presented Lear with the Collier Trophy in 1950. Years later, a French Caravelle airliner made history by conducting a series of completely blind (unprogrammed by the pilot) landings with the Lear Autopilot.

Throughout the 1940s and '50s, the Lear name had become synonymous with aircraft controls and instrumentation. During the early '50s, Lear would begin a project that would inspire him to his most widely known product: the business jet. His quest began with converting a dual-engine Lockheed Lodestar into a more aerodynamic plane with a luxury interior, and the first flight of the Learstar in 1954 achieved a top speed of 320 miles per hour (40 miles per hour higher than the original Lockheed model). Sixty Learstars were sold—a respectable number for the period but far short of Lear's goal.

As the Lear Corporation grew to five thousand employees in America and overseas in the late 1950s and early 1960s, Lear found himself spending an inordinate amount of time flying from destination to destination. This trend was compounded when he moved his family to Geneva, Switzerland, in 1960. He believed that the future of air travel would be by jet and that a business jet that was faster, lighter and less expensive than a converted Lockheed was what the market needed. When he presented the idea to his board of directors, however, he was voted down. The stated reasons were that development costs would run too high and that the market would be too crowded by the time the jet would be available to the public.

Lear could not set aside his vision for the business jet, and he arranged for Lear, Inc., to purchase his shares in the firm for a total of $15 million to help finance his new venture, Lear Jet, Inc. Using the technology of the Swiss P-16 fighter, he moved his headquarters to Wichita, Kansas (at the Municipal Airport), to build a factory in 1962. He was able to set up a mass production line for the jet and tested the first finished Lear Jet in the fall of 1963, all the while funding the entire process—from design to finished product—by himself without bank support. The finished product became the first mass-produced business jet aircraft, setting transcontinental records and becoming a leader in non-military jet sales by 1967, the year Lear Jet, Inc., was acquired by the Gates Rubber Company for $30 million.

During this same time frame, Lear had been looking for a reliable way to offer music in his new business jets. He had examined a four-track magnetic tape cartridge with an endless loop design first marketed by Fidelipac and then adapted for stereo by Earl "Madman" Muntz in 1962. Lear had liked the four-track, quarter-inch tape system and started to carry them in his jets, only to be dissatisfied with the limitations of the Muntz technology. He contacted the suppliers of the equipment tape heads and experimented with smaller heads, pressure rollers and track spacing to enable eight stereo tracks on one cartridge. This became known as the "Stereo-8" player, which was unveiled in 1964 to several car companies and RCA. Since the player was designed with just a couple of knobs for controls, it could be operated from a moving vehicle without distraction. RCA agreed to release its catalogue on Learjet Stereo-8 cartridges, which led to Ford's commitment to offer the player as optional equipment on 1966 models. Sixty-five thousand players were installed that year. The eight-track player, as unfashionable as it appears in retrospect, was the dominant format for portable music playback until the end of the 1970s.

Lear's one major business misstep started after leaving Lear Jet, Inc. He bought a facility in Reno, Nevada, to develop a pollution-free engine, one that was based on a steam- and vapor-driven turbine model. While he succeeded in creating the engine, the efficiency and power—or lack of it— made his finished product impractical at the time. In the process, he lost millions of dollars, since, like with the Lear Jet project, he had financed the business with only his own money.

In the mid-1970s, besides developing a twelve-passenger jet called the Challenger 600, Lear launched a project that would be his last: the Learfan 2100. He was inspired to design the seven-passenger Learfan in an attempt to find new ways for jets to consume less fuel, which was rising in price quickly at the time. The aircraft was to be built from composite materials instead of aluminum (comparable to a carbon-fiber type of technology) and powered by two turboprop engines. Even after being diagnosed with leukemia in early 1978, Lear guided his employees to complete the design and set up production. He died two months after his diagnosis on May 14, but his wife, Moya, continued the building of a prototype after his death at his insistence. The aircraft worked but could not gain FAA certification and was thus never put into production.

Some biographies mention that Lear's private life was at odds with his public profile as a trailblazing businessman, claiming that he was a difficult person to work or live with at times. A hint at his personality can be found in an interview on business ownership, where he was quoted as saying, "If you put up half of the money, you get to make half of the decisions." Perhaps this reasoning is why he stayed in partnerships only for short periods of time and funded his biggest projects without outside involvement.

Among many honorary degrees, fellowships and awards, Hannibal Regional Airport renamed itself, in 2003, the Hannibal Regional Airport, William P. Lear Field.

George Coleman Poage

James and Annie Poage welcomed the birth of their second son, George Coleman, on November 6, 1880. At the time, the Poage family lived in Hannibal, where all three of their children, including George, were born. James was a former slave; Annie is said to have been a free woman before the Civil War.

It is recorded that the Poage family relocated to La Crosse, Wisconsin, in 1884, when James was offered work as a tanner for A.W. Pettibone. It is possible that James was transferred there after working for Pettibone's son, Wilson B. Pettibone of Hannibal.

La Crosse was a vibrant and prosperous city for both whites and blacks in the mid-1880s. Educational opportunities were available to all, and George

Poage was able to attend La Crosse High School. He was a good student and posted outstanding marks in his classes.

He was a gifted athlete as well. On May 29, 1899, during a track meet against Winona, Minnesota, Poage placed first in the 50-yard dash, the 100-yard dash and the 220-yard dash. He then removed his shoes and claimed second place in the standing broad jump. In 1913, a La Crosse newspaper would describe Poage as "one of the fastest men in [the] world at [that] time" and "perhaps the greatest track athlete that was ever developed in this city."

George Poage was the first African American to graduate from La Crosse High School. He was ranked second in his class of twenty-five students and gave the salutatorian address at the graduation commencement ceremony on June 23, 1899.

After graduation, Poage matriculated to the University of Wisconsin–Madison (UW), where he ran for the varsity track team beginning in his sophomore year. He was the first African American to compete for the

George Poage (left, bottom row) posing with his University of Wisconsin team in 1903, one year before becoming the first African American to win a medal in a modern Olympiad. *Courtesy Steven Dast/University of Wisconsin–Madison.*

university's team, specializing in short sprints and hurdles. In 1902, the student newspaper, the *Daily Cardinal*, reported that "while [varsity head coach] Kilpatrick is absent, Mr. Poage will take charge of the track work."

Poage graduated from the university in 1903. His senior thesis in history was entitled "An Investigation into the Economic Condition of the Negro in the State of Georgia During the Period 1860–1900." He returned to UW in the fall of 1903 and was employed by the university's football team as a trainer while taking graduate-level courses in history. In June 1904, Poage became the first African American track and field champion in Big Ten Conference history, placing first in both the 440-yard dash and the 220-yard hurdles.

In 1904, the Olympic Games were to be held during the World's Fair in St. Louis, Missouri. Controversy surrounded the fair, with prominent African American leaders protesting against racial segregation policies by the fair's officials. The Olympiad's attendees would be segregated, as the organizers of the World's Fair had built separate facilities for black and white spectators. African American leaders from all across the country called for a boycott of the competition. Despite the boycott, 645 men and 6 women from twelve countries participated in the 1904 Olympic Games.

Poage was sponsored by the Milwaukee Athletic Club to compete in the 1904 Games and decided to attend. He went on to place third in both the 220- and 440-yard hurdles, becoming the first African American to earn a medal in a modern Olympiad.

After receiving his bronze Olympic medals, Poage decided to stay in St. Louis. He became a teacher at Sumner High School, where he would later be named chair of the English Department. He also coached several of the school's sports teams.

After World War I, Poage moved to Chicago. There were few job opportunities available to African Americans during the 1920s. In 1924, Poage accepted a position as a clerk for the United States Post Office and continued to work there for more than thirty years. He died in Chicago on April 11, 1962, at the age of eighty-one. In 1998, he was honored by being inducted to the Wisconsin Athletic Hall of Fame in Milwaukee.

Ron Powers

Nearly one hundred years after young Sammy Clemens frolicked as a child along the shores of the Mississippi, so too did another gifted writer. Ron Powers was born in Hannibal in 1941, and throughout his childhood, he watched his hometown celebrate the legacy of its favorite son, Mark Twain.

It did not take long for Powers to receive similar recognition and accolades from friends and loved ones in Hannibal. Early in his career, Powers became the 1973 Pulitzer Prize winner for criticism while writing for the *Chicago-Sun Times*. He was the first television critic to be so honored.

In 1985, Powers would win an Emmy award for the CBS show *Sunday Morning*, where he contributed film, book and drama reviews from 1979 to 1988.

His first book, *Newscasters: The News Business as Show Business*, was published in 1979 by St. Martin's Press. His hometown would be the subject of his next nonfiction work, *White Town Drowsing: Journeys to Hannibal*, published by Atlantic Monthly Press in 1986. Three other books featuring Hannibal would follow: *Dangerous Water: A Biography of the Boy Who Became Mark Twain* (1999), *Tom and Huck Don't Live Here Anymore: Childhood and Murder in the Heart of America* (2001) and *Mark Twain: A Life* (2005).

In 2000, Powers would coauthor with James Bradley *Flags of Our Fathers*, a nonfiction account of men serving at Iwo Jima during World War II. *Flags of Our Fathers* would spend forty-six weeks on the *New York Times* bestseller list (six weeks at number one). The book was adapted for the 2006 film of the same name, produced by Steven Spielberg and directed by Clint Eastwood.

True Compass, the 2009 autobiography of Senator Ted Kennedy in which he discussed his life as a public servant and member of the legendary Kennedy family, was ghostwritten by Ron Powers. Kennedy personally selected Powers to assist him with the project, which took more than five years to complete.

The year 2010 was the 175th anniversary of Twain's birth, the 100th anniversary of his death and the 150th anniversary of the publishing of *Adventures of Huckleberry Finn*. To celebrate these milestones, Powers added "playwright" to his resume by penning *Sam and Laura*, a two-act play dramatizing an encounter between Sam Clemens and Laura Wright (a possible candidate for the inspiration of the character Becky Thatcher). Powers offered the play royalty-free to any amateur or professional group that wished to stage it during the 2010 "Year of Twain."

In addition to writing, Powers has taught at the Bread Loaf Writers' Conference in Vermont (called by the *New Yorker* "the oldest and most prestigious writers' conference in the country"), at the Salzburg Seminar in Austria and at Middlebury College in Middlebury, Vermont.

At the time of this writing, Powers resides with his wife, Honoree, in Castleton, Vermont.

HAROLD VOLKMER

Jefferson City, Missouri, was the birthplace of Harold L. Volkmer. He was born on April 4, 1931, and spent his childhood in the shadow of the Missouri state capitol. Volkmer attended Jefferson City Junior College and Saint Louis University and received his law degree from the University of Missouri–Columbia in 1955.

Volkmer served in the United States Army from 1955 to 1957. After his return, he set up a private law practice in Hannibal, where he also served

Former congressman Harold Volkmer. *Courtesy Quincy Herald-Whig.*

as an assistant Missouri attorney general. In 1960, Volkmer was elected prosecuting attorney for Marion County.

Volkmer was elected to the Missouri House of Representatives in 1966 and served four terms. As chairman of the Missouri House Judiciary Committee, Volkmer sought and obtained approval of the Equal Rights Amendment by the Missouri House of Representatives in 1975.

In 1976, Volkmer was elected to the United States House of Representatives. He would be reelected nine times as the Ninth District representative from Missouri.

Following in the footsteps of William H. Hatch, Harold Volkmer served on the House Agriculture Committee, assisting in the writing of five major farm bills. He was also appointed to the House Judiciary Committee. His progressive ideology led him to support the creation of the Department of Education, civil rights legislation, environmental laws and the Panama Canal Treaty. Although a Democrat, Volkmer broke with party lines in his opposition to gun control and abortion legislation. In 1986, Volkmer cosponsored the Firearm Owners Protection Act, which amended the previous Gun Control Act, allowing compliance inspections of retailers selling firearms.

Harold Volkmer was defeated in his reelection bid in 1996. After leaving Congress, he was elected to the board of the National Rifle Association and also served as chairman of the National Commission on Small Arms. Volkmer continues to live in Hannibal at the time of this writing.

BIBLIOGRAPHY

Abandoned Rails. "The Hannibal and Saint Joseph Railroad." www. abandonedrails.com/Hannibal_and_Saint_Joseph_Railroad.

Andrews, Gregg. *City of Dust: A Cement Company Town in the Land of Tom Sawyer.* Columbia: University of Missouri Press, 1996

Answers.com. "Gale Encyclopedia of US History: Boot and Shoe Manufacturing." www.answers.com/topic/boot-and-shoe-manufacturing.

Bacon, Thomas H. *Mirror of Hannibal 1905.* Revised and reprinted by J. Hurley and Roberta (Roland) Hagood. Hannibal, MO: Hannibal Free Public Library/Jostens (Marceline, MO), 1990.

———. "1901 Encyclopedia of the History of Missouri: Marion County." Rootsweb: Ancestry.com. www.rootsweb.ancestry. com/~momarion/1901hist.htm.

Baron, Jane. "A Brief History of Shoe Manufacturing, Part One." Article Alley. www.articlealley.com/article_1201713_34.html.

Baseball Almanac. "Major League Baseball Players Born in Missouri." www. baseball-almanac.com/players/birthplace.php?loc=Missouri.

Baseball-Reference.com. "Jake Beckley Statistics and History." www. baseball-reference.com/players/b/becklja01.shtml.

Biographical Directory of the United States Congress, 1774–2005. "William Henry Hatch." Washington, D.C.: Joint Committee on Printing Congress, 2006.

Boesen, Victor. *They Said It Couldn't Be Done: The Incredible Story of Bill Lear.* New York: Doubleday & Co., 1971.

Brewer, Jim. "Welcome Back Cotton." *Fastbreak Magazine* (March 1996). Available online at www.nba.com/suns/history/cotton_fastbreak_march96.html.

Brown, Thomas J. *American Eras: Civil War and Reconstruction, 1850–1877.* New York: Manly, Inc., 1997.

Bryant, Eliza. "The New Madrid Earthquake." http://hsv.com/genlintr/newmadrd/accnt1.htm.

Captains of Industry. "Pierre Laclede." Literature Collection. www.literaturecollection.com/a/james-parton/captains-of-industry/11.

Christensen, Lawrence O., William E. Foley, Gary E. Kremer and Kenneth H. Winn, eds. *Dictionary of Missouri Biography.* Columbia: University of Missouri Press, 1999.

Christman, Margaret C.S. *1846: Portrait of the Nation.* Washington, D.C.: Smithsonian Institution, 1996.

Colton, G. Woolworth. *Map of the Hannibal & St. Joseph Railroad and Its Connections.* New York: American Railway Review, 1860

Coontz, Robert E., *From the Mississippi to the Sea,* Philadelphia: Dorrance & Company, Inc., 1930.

Dempsey, Terrell. *Searching for Jim: Slavery in Sam Clemens's World.* Columbia: University of Missouri Press, 2003.

Dreker, John. "Pirates Prospects: Alleghenys Strike Gold." www.piratesprospects.com/2011/01/alleghenys-strike-gold.html.

Enchanted Learning. "Rene-Robert Cavelier, Sieur de La Salle: North American Explorer." www.enchantedlearning.com/explorers/page/l/lasalle.shtml.

Encyclopedia of World Biography, s.v. "William Henry Hatch." Encyclopedia.com. www.encyclopedia.com/doc/1G2-3404702839.html.

Everything2.com. "William Lear." http://everything2.com/title/William+Lear.

Famous Belgians. "Louis Hennepin." www.famousbelgians.net/hennepin.htm.

Fielder, David. *The Enemy Among Us: POWs in Missouri During World War II.* St. Louis: Missouri Historical Society Press, 2003

Fleitz, David. "The Baseball Biography Project: Jake Beckley." http://bioproj.sabr.org/bioproj.cfm?a=v&v=l&pid=829&bid=972.

Green, Harvey. *The Uncertainty of Everyday Life, 1915–1945,* Fayetteville: University of Arkansas Press, 2000.

Hagood, J. Hurley, and Roberta Hagood. *Hannibal, Too: Historic Sketches of Hannibal and Its Neighbors*. Marceline, MO: Walsworth Publishing Co., 1986.

———. *Hannibal Flood '93*. Hannibal, MO: Courier-Post, 1995.

———. *Hannibal's Yesterdays*. Marceline, MO: Jostens Publishing, 1992.

———. *The Story of Hannibal: A Bicentennial History, 1976*. Hannibal, MO: The Hannibal Free Public Library/Standard Printing Co., 1976.

Hagood, J. Hurley, Roberta Hagood and Dave Thomson. *Hannibal Heritage*. Marceline, MO: Heritage House Publishing, 1994.

Hagood, J. Hurley, Roberta Hagood and Mary Lou Montgomery. *Hannibal Bridges the Mississippi*. Marceline, MO: Jostens Publishing, 2000.

Hannibal Courier-Post. "Hannibal Has a Rich Heritage of River Life, Adventurous Settlers." 1938. Aailable online at http://visithannibalmo.com/visit/historicalnews/river_life.shtml.

Hannibal Historic Societies. "Friends of Historic Hannibal." Marion County, MO and Hannibal, MO Historic Groups. www.hannibalhistoricsocieties.org/FOHH.htm.

Hill, Edwin L., and Bruce L. Mouser. "George Coleman Poage: His LaCrosse, Wisconsin Years, 1885–1904." Digitized Resources: Murphy Library, University of Wisconsin–LaCrosse. http://murphylibrary.uwlax.edu/digital/lacrosse/poage/00030003.htm.

Hilton, Ronald. "What's In a Name?" www.stanford.edu/group/wais/History/history_hannibal.htm.

Historic Earthquakes. "New Madrid Earthquakes 1811–1812." http://earthquake.usgs.gov/earthquakes/states/events/1811-1812.php.

"History: City of Galena." City of Galena. www.cityofgalena.org/history.cfm.

History of Recorded Technology. "Bill Lear Invents the 8-Track and Brings in Ford, Motorola, and RCA Victor." Recording History. www.recording-history.org/HTML/8track4.php.

Hoebing, Phil. "Legends of Lovers Leaps." *Missouri Folklore Society Journal* 21 (1999): 81–98. Available online at www.qufriary.org/Hoebing/lleap.html.

Holcombe, R.I. *History of Marion County Missouri*. St. Louis, MO: E.F. Perkins, 1884.

Internet Movie Database. "Cliff Edwards." www.imdb.com/name/nm0249893.

———. "*Flags of Our Fathers*." www.imdb.com/title/tt0418689.

———. "*Titanic*." www.imdb.com/title/tt0120338.

Iversen, Kristen. *Molly Brown: Unraveling the Myth*. Boulder, CO: Johnson Printing, 1999.

Jazz Age 1920s. "Cliff Edwards: Biography." www.jazzage1920s.com/ cliffedwards/biography/biography.php.

Jensen, Oliver. *The American Heritage History of Railroads in America*. New York: American Heritage Publishing Co., Inc., 1975.

Kilbane, Doris. "William Lear: Aviation Legend Makes Waves In Audio, Too." Electronic Design. http://electronicdesign.com/article/communications/ william-lear-aviation-legend-makes-waves-in-audio-aspx.

Kiner, Larry F. *The Cliff Edwards Discography*. Westport, CT: Greenwood Press, Inc., 1987.

Kluth, Andreas. "Hannibal, Fabius, and Scipio in Missouri." The Hannibal Blog. http://andreaskluth.org/2010/05/13/hannibal- fabius-scipio-in-missouri.

Lake Gazette. "25th Anniversary of Dam Being Observed." www.monroecity. net/archives_articles.asp?xissuedate=090812.

Lear Family Trust. "William P Lear.com." http://williamplear.com/bio_ovw.html.

Lee, George R. *Slavery North of St. Louis*. Canton, MO: Lewis County Historical Society, 2000.

Legends of the Dead-Ball Era. "Forgotten Heroes of the Dead-Ball Era." http://baseballcards.galib.uga.edu/forgotten-heroes/?Welcome&Welcome.

Life. "Roll of Honor." March 30, 1942.

Lotz, David. "The CB&Q Mark Twain Zephyr." *Rail Merchants International*. www.railmerchants.net/mt-zephyr.htm.

McClure, C.H. *History of Missouri*. Chicago: Laidlaw Brothers, Inc., 1920.

McLachlan, Sean. *Missouri: An Illustrated History*. New York: Hippocrene Books, Inc., 2008.

Missouri Bureau of Labor Statistics. *Missouri, 1912–13–14: Resources, Advantages, and Opportunities of a Thriving Commonwealth*. Jefferson City, MO: Hugh Stevens Publishing Co., 1914.

Missouri State Archives and Charter Media. "Marie Byrum Video Transcript." *Moments in Missouri Political History Video Segments*. www.sos.mo.gov/mdh/ mmh/transcripts/mmph_tsByrum.html?Submit=View+Transcript.

Modelski, Andrew W. *Railroad Maps of North America: The First Hundred Years*. Washington, D.C.: Library of Congress, 1984.

MoGenWeb. "Hannibal Shoe Factories." www.rootsweb.ancestry. com/~momarion/hannibalshoefactory.htm.

Motorola. "Music in Motion: The First Motorola-Branded Car Radio." www.motorola.com/Consumers/US-EN/About_Motorola/History/ Explore_Motorola_Heritage/Music_In_Motion.

Musick, John Roy. *Stories of Missouri*. New York: American Book Company, 1897.

National Baseball Hall of Fame and Museum. "Beckley, Jake." http://baseballhall.org/hof/beckley-jake.

19th Century Baseball. "Baseball History: Evolution of 19th Century Baseball Rules." http://www.19cbaseball.com/rules-3.html.

Oster, Donald B. "The Hannibal and St. Joseph Railroad, Government and Town Funding, 1846–1861." *Missouri Historical Review* 87, no. 4 (July 1993): 403–21.

Overton, Richard C. *Burlington Route: A History of the Burlington Lines*. New York: Alfred A. Knopf, 1965.

Parrish, William E. *Turbulent Partnership: Missouri and the Union, 1861–1865*, Columbia: University of Missouri Press, 1963.

Penick, James L. *The New Madrid Earthquakes*. Columbia: University of Missouri Press, 1981.

"Pierre Laclede Ligest." *Lewis and Clark Journey of Discovery*. www.nps.gov/archive/jeff/LewisClark2/Circa1804/StLouis/blockinfo/Block34ALaclede.htm.

Powers, Ron. *Mark Twain: A Life*. New York: Free Press, 2005.

———. "Sam and Laura." www.samandlauraplay.com.

Price, Steve. "Redleg Nation: September 26, This Day in Reds History." http://redlegnation.com/2010/09/26/this-day-in-reds-history-road-trip-jake-beckley-walks-haunt-and-playoff-hopes.

Prokopowicz, Gerald J. *American Eras: The Reform Era and Eastern U. S. Development, 1815–1850*, New York: Manly, Inc., 1998.

Ramsay, Robert Lee. *Our Storehouse of Missouri Place Names*. Columbia: University of Missouri Press, 1952.

Sampson, Wade. "From Ukelele Ike to Jiminy Cricket: Cliff Edwards." *MousePlanet*. www.mouseplanet.com/9135/From_Ukelele_Ike_to_Jiminy_Cricket_Cliff_Edwards.

Schlereth, Thomas J. *Victorian America: Transformations in Everyday Life, 1876–1915*. New York: HarperCollins Publishers, Inc., 1991.

State Historical Society of Missouri. "One Hundredth Anniversary of the First Railway Postal Car Observed in Hannibal." *Missouri Historical Review* 57, no. 1 (October 1962): 93–98.

Stover, John F. *The Routledge Historical Atlas of the American Railroads*. New York: Routledge, 1999.

Time. "Nelson Takes Over." February 21, 1941.

Truman Area Community Network. "Encyclopedia of the History of Missouri: Railroad Articles." http://tacnet.missouri.org/history/encycmo/encycmorr.html.

Twain, Mark. *Adventures of Huckleberry Finn: The Only Comprehensive Edition.* Foreword and Addendum by Victor Doyno. New York: Random House, 1996.

———. *The Adventures of Tom Sawyer.* New York: Oxford University Press, 1996.

———. *Following the Equator.* New York: Oxford University Press, 1996.

———. *The Innocents Abroad.* New York: Oxford University Press, 1996.

———. *Life on the Mississippi.* New York: Oxford University Press, 1996.

———. *Old Times on the Mississippi.* New York: Oxford University Press, 1996.

Twain, Mark, and Charles Dudley Warner. *The Gilded Age.* New York: Quill Pen Classics, 2008.

"Twain's Life and Works." Mark Twain Boyhood Home & Museum. www.marktwainmuseum.org/index.php/research/twains-life-and-works.

United States Court of Customs and Patent Appeals. *Elder Mfg. Co. v. International Shoe Co., Patent Appeal No. 5834* (1952). 194 F.2d 114.

United States Department of the Interior Heritage Conservation and Recreation Service. "National Register of Historic Places Inventory-Nomination Form: Federal Building." Department of Natural Resources. www.dnr.mo.gov/shpo/nps-nr/80002377.pdf.

Ward, Geoffrey C., and Ken Burns. *Baseball: An Illustrated History.* New York: Alfred A. Knopf, Inc., 1994.

Ward, Geoffrey C., and Ric Burns. *The Civil War: An Illustrated History.* New York: Alfred A. Knopf, Inc., 1990.

Weaver, H. Dwight. *Missouri Caves in History and Legend.* Columbia: University of Missouri Press, 2008.

Wikipedia. "George Coleman Poage." http://en.wikipedia.org/wiki/George_Poage.

———. "Great White Fleet." http://en.wikipedia.org/wiki/Great_White_Fleet.

———. "Hannibal and St. Joseph Railroad." http://en.wikipedia.org/wiki/Hannibal_and_St._Joseph_Railroad.

———. "Jacques Marquette." http://en.wikipedia.org/wiki/Jacques_Marquette.

———. "Jake Beckley." http://en.wikipedia.org/wiki/Jake_Beckley.

—————. "Louis Hennepin." http://en.wikipedia.org/wiki/Louis_Hennepin.

—————. "Soulard, St. Louis." http://en.wikipedia.org/wiki/Soulard,_St._Louis.

—————. "Steamboats of the Mississippi." http://en.wikipedia.org/wiki/Steamboats_of_the_Mississippi.

Williams, Walter, ed. *A History of Northeast Missouri*. 3 vols. Chicago: Lewis Publishing Co., 1913.

Young, Anthony. "The Vision of William P. Lear." *Freeman*. www.thefreemanonline.org/featured/the-vision-of-william-p-lear.

Zimmermann, Karl. *Burlington's Zephyrs*. St. Paul, MN: MBI Publishing Company, 2004.

INDEX

ABOUT THE AUTHORS

Ken and Lisa Marks are curators of the Hannibal History Museum, conduct Haunted Hannibal Ghost Tours™ and are contributors to publications such as *Hannibal Magazine* and *Missouri Life*. Lifelong history fanatics, they are committed to the preservation of Hannibal's natural, cultural and industrial heritage and are members of the Friends of Historic Hannibal, the Marion County [Missouri] Historical Society and the Historic Hannibal Marketing Council. They are lovingly restoring their 1885 Second Empire home located in the nationally recognized Central Park Historic District of Hannibal. Their first book, *Haunted Hannibal: History and Mystery in America's Hometown*, was published by The History Press in September 2010.

Visit us at
www.historypress.net

.

.